W9-ADN-263

# What Book Reviewers Said About
## *Black Fatherhood: The Guide to Male Parenting*

"This well-written book fills a special need for black fathers."

*Library Journal*

"Dr. ⟨...⟩ empha-sis o⟨...⟩

Ron Charles, *Ebony Man*

"This is a book about what black fathers are doing right."
Herb Boyd, *Black Enterprise*

"What I found most refreshing is to hear black men talk for the first time about their experiences of being a father."
Kenneth H. Bonnell, *Players Magazine*

"Hutchinson shows in his book that the male presence is very strong in many African-American homes."
Dorothy Gilliam, *Washington Post*

"*Black Fatherhood* describes the unique challenges of being a black dad."           Marc Lacey, *Los Angeles Times*

"*Black Fatherhood* explores the special concerns and problems of black fathers."           *Ebony Magazine*

"*Black Fatherhood* presents information and advice offered by black men to black men."
V.R. Peterson, *Essence Magazine*

JUN 20 1996

"*Black Fatherhood* is a unique approach to a complex problem."

Larry Aubry, *Los Angeles Sentinel*

"*Black Fatherhood* is good tonic for those who believe that black men are getting a bad rap."

*Atlanta Daily World*

"Dr. Hutchinson is out to set the record straight on black males." *Philadelphia News Observer*

ꟻEB 2 0 1995

# Black Fatherhood

## The Guide to Male Parenting

Earl Ofari Hutchinson, Ph.D.

MIDDLE PASSAGE PRESS
Los Angeles, CA 90043

© 1995 by Earl Ofari Hutchinson
Fifth Printing

© Cover Illustration by Lightbourne Images

All rights reserved.

Published by:
MIDDLE PASSAGE PRESS
5517 Secrest Drive
Los Angeles, CA 90043
(213) 298-0266

Printed and bound in the United States of America

Hutchinson, Earl Ofari, 1945-
    Black fatherhood: a guide to male parenting / Earl
Ofari Hutchinson.
    p. cm.
    Includes bibliographical references and index.
    ISBN 1-881032-09-4
    1. Fatherhood--United States--Afro-Americans--Guide
books. 2. Parenting--United States--Guide-books. 3.
Father and child--United States. I. Title.

HQ756.H8 1992                          306.8742
                                       92-71110

BOOKS BY DR. EARL OFARI HUTCHINSON

*The Myth of Black Capitalism*
*Let Your Motto Be Resistance*
*The Mugging of Black America*
*Black Fatherherhood II: Black Women Talk*
*About Their Men*
*The Assassination of the Black Male Image*
*Blacks and Reds: Race and Class in Conflict, 1919-1990*

HOLYOKE COMMUNITY COLLEGE
ELAINE NICPON MARIEB LIBRARY

## Author's Note

I don't promise any magic formulas for being a black father. I promise only to present situations and problems that confront black fathers. I promise that the fathers you will meet in **Black Fatherhood** will tell you how they dealt with their own problems.

If you expect this book to tell you what black men are doing wrong, CLOSE IT NOW! You can find that anywhere. This is a book that tells you what they are doing right.

*To my family and to all African American families who strive daily to raise their children to be responsible, productive and creative human beings.*

ACKNOWLEDGMENTS

I wish to thank the people who have read my manuscript and provided critical and substantive comments: Larry Aubry, Dr. John Henrik Clarke, Dr. Sandra Cox, Joye Day, Yvonne Divans, Dr. Gloria Haithman-Ali, Dr. George J. McKenna, III, Roland H. Lockett, Ph.D., Alvin F. Poussaint, MD, and Stephanie Sharp.

A special thanks to my wife, Barbara Hutchinson, who's love, encouragement and hard work helped to make *Black Fatherhood* a reality.

Special thanks to Moorland-Spingarn Research Center, Howard University for permission to use the illustration "The Hunted Slaves."

Cover illustration "A Moment In Time" by Albert Fennell © 1994

Cover Illustration is available through Paloma Editions
1-800-321-2053.

# CONTENTS

# FOREWORD

The news media often gives the impression that concerned black fathers are rare. There are numerous articles on "disappearing black fathers," and social science has concentrated its studies on *single* black mothers. Black men, however, know that their roles have not been adequately presented.

*Black Fatherhood* is a pleasure to read because it considers what African-American fathers are doing *right* for a change. Dr. Hutchinson uses his own and others' experiences to describe and illuminate their experience of fatherhood. Using examples and straight-forward language, this book provides advice and support for black fathers.

This readable volume encourages active involvement of fathers with their children. Dr. Hutchinson emphasizes the many ways we can support our children's healthy development without spending a lot of money. He also provides suggestions for staying involved with your children even if you live apart from the family. Dr. Hutchinson disputes the many excuses men have offered for non-involvement and offers a common sense approach to discipline and education.

This book takes a strong stand that men belong in the home, taking an equal role with women in homemaking and child care. I recommend this book for all citizens who wish to strengthen the black family.

Alvin F. Poussaint, MD
Clinical Professor of Psychiatry
Harvard Medical School, Boston

Moorland-Spingarn Research Center, Howard University

The Hunted Slaves (1865) Engraved by C. G. Lewis

# INTRODUCTION: HOW THEY ARE SEEN

*I think the biggest problem is how society looks at black men and how black men look at themselves.*

Robert, a black father

"Ain't I a woman too?" In 1853 Abolitionist leader Sojourner Truth asked this question. She knew that American society did not regard a black woman as a woman. The question could be easily asked today about black fathers. "Ain't I a father too?" To many Americans, the black father is like Ralph Ellison's "Invisible Man." He's a body they don't see, a voice they don't hear, and a person they don't know.

Browse through any bookstore and count how many books there are on black fathers. I did. There were none. In the growing number of books on fathering, there were no specific references to the problems of black fathers. Yet, in those same books there were chapters on "single fathers," "gay fathers," "teen fathers," "step fathers," "adoptive fathers," "new fathers" and "old fathers."

In the books on fatherhood, dozens of organizations, support groups and councils for fathers were mentioned. There were no listings for organizations or support groups that deal with the special needs and problems of black fathers. The books listed a variety of tapes, videos, films, magazines, as well as news and feature articles on the problems of fathers. Again, only a handful concerned black men. And none focused on black men as fathers.

Even black publications such as *Essence, Ebony* and *Jet* have published only occasional articles that focused exclusively on black fathers. The books by black writers are mostly recountings of personal remembrances of their own fathers.

I was hardly surprised by this. American society wrapped its tight cloak of invisibility around black fatherhood during slavery. Wives were separated from their husbands. Children were brutally torn from their parents and sold. Most slave masters considered marriage a nuisance and they discouraged it. If that was true, then how could black families be families? How could black fathers be fathers? Many were.

*...i long to hear from my family how the ar geten along you will ples to let me no how the ar geten along...for god sake let me hear from you all my wife and children are not out of my mine nor night.*
> Testimony of Thomas Ducket,
> a runaway slave

No heroic sagas or tales were written about these men. No tributes were paid to them. So the myth grew that they did not exist. But they did. Black fathers had families. And they cared about them. Black fathers took great risks and made sacrifices to free their wives and children from bondage. Some physically rescued them. Others purchased them. They were driven by a sense of loyalty and love. They were desperate to fulfill their responsibilities as fathers.

Following emancipation, they made their marriages legal. So many that in one North Carolina county a former slave woman complained: "Everybody's getting married and my old man can't get the money."

She was not exaggerating:

*I Elbert William & Marien Williams has been livin together 18 years & We both do affirm that We do want each other to Live as man & wife the balance of Life....*

For decades after slavery, African-Americans married and raised their families the same as other Americans. In Harlem in 1925, more than six out of seven black homes had two parents. In 1960, more than 80 percent of blacks were married and living together.

And then came sociologist Daniel Patrick Moynihan. Under White House tutelage in 1965, he published his enduring report, *The Negro Family: The Case for National Action.* After what he claimed was an exhaustive check of all the facts and figures on the black family structure, he pronounced his verdict: The black family was "a tangle of pathology." Why? Because there were too few fathers in the home.

Many politicians and much of the press believed him. The black father became their perfect foil for America's neglect of the black poor. If blacks were destitute, it was because black men deserted the home. If blacks committed crime, it was because black men were ignorant and irresponsible. If blacks took drugs and were abusive, it was because black men had no sense of self-worth. If they failed, it was their own fault.

Many blacks challenged Moynihan. They accused him of juggling figures, using faulty research methods and of ignoring the three out of four black men that were not absent fathers. But Moynihan prevailed. Black fathers were now officially labeled "derelict." Many Americans refused to believe Dr. Martin Luther King, Jr.:

*The Negro was crushed, battered and brutalized, but he never gave up. He proves again that life is stronger than death. The Negro family is scarred; it is submerged; but it struggles to survive.*

Often myths become reality. The reality for many black families is that black men do desert their homes. They make babies that they don't take care of. They fill the jails and prisons. They join gangs and commit acts of violence. They die young from drugs, alcohol and disease. From conception to adulthood they are forced to run the gantlet of American abuses.

That's part of the story. Many black fathers do stay in the home. They sacrifice to provide the necessities for their wives and children. They overcome mountainous obstacles to build strong relationships with their loved ones. They roll up their sleeves, put their chin to the grindstone and go forward.

Black fathers want their sons to smile into the camera on the sidelines of football games, wave and say, "Hi dad." They are men like my father who, as he nears the ninth decade of his life, looked me in the eye and said, "My children have been my life, never forget that." I didn't.

My father stood on the firm foundation of history and tradition. He drew strength from black leaders like Henry Highland Garnet, Martin Delaney, Frederick Douglass, W.E.B. DuBois, Booker T. Washington, Marcus Garvey, A. Phillip Randolph, Paul Robeson, Malcolm X, Martin Luther King, Jr. and Elijah Muhammad. Their contributions have enriched not only the black experience, but America's social tapestry. They were fathers who never lost sight of the importance of family.

***Black Fatherhood*** is a book about fathers who enriched their families. The men I interviewed span several generations. They have different incomes and occupations. They are married, separated and divorced. They raise their children alone. They know the joy and pain of close relationships. They experience poverty and prosperity. They face discrimination. They confront violence, gangs, drugs and sexual risks. They make hard choices about their children's education, health and welfare. They tell how they are bringing their families through the gantlet of American problems. At the end of **Black Fatherhood**, you will find the complete list of questions that I asked each man.

**Black Fatherhood** is not a book about defeatism and despair. It is a book about optimism and hope. It is a book about success. It is a book that finally lifts the cloak of invisibility from black fathers.

In **Black Fatherhood** six men tell what it means to be a black father in America. I will let them introduce themselves. The names have been changed to protect their privacy.

● ● ● ● ● ●

My name is Perry. I am twenty six years old. I work for an aerospace company as an estimator. I have a son who is three and a daughter, six.

I never thought that I had an especially hard life growing up in Denver. Even though I didn't really know my father, my mother did the best she could. My brothers and sisters never went without anything.

In high school, I did most of the things that fellows my age do, played a little basketball, fooled around with the girls and tried to have a good time.

After I graduated, I wasn't ready for college. So I joined the Navy. I learned a few skills, travelled a lot and pretty much enjoyed myself. When I got out I got married. Unfortunately, the marriage didn't last. We drifted apart.

After we broke up, the kids lived with their mother. At the time, I thought that was best. But, after a while, I wanted to play more of a role in their lives so we arranged to have joint custody. I can honestly say that raising two small children alone is quite an experience. It requires an adjustment. I had to make some changes, but it worked out.

Now I'm back in school studying engineering. I also remarried and we're expecting a child. My family is growing, so that's another challenge, but I think it's a challenge I'll enjoy facing.

● ● ● ● ● ●

My name is Robert. I am thirty-five years old. I'm a high school music teacher in Compton, California. I have three sons. They are aged seventeen, twelve and seven.

I only met my father one time, for an hour when I

was fifteen. I was practically raised by my aunt and uncle in Los Angeles. They didn't have a lot, and there were a few rough times. But we still managed to get by.

Early on, I fell in love with music. I tried a lot of instruments and I think I have become pretty proficient on the piano and trumpet. In college, music was my major. I've been fortunate, I'm able to make a little extra money playing parties and social events on the week-ends.

Also, I was able to live in West Africa for two years. This was really an eye opener for me about my people and their culture. It was a good experience and I learned a lot.

I got married in my early twenties. It's still painful to admit it, but after all the years my wife and I were together we realized that we wanted different things, so we separated. But I knew that I was going to take care of my sons because I believe strongly that boys should be with their fathers.

I have remarried and my wife and I are expecting. Who knows, this time my sons may have to make room for a sister.

• • • • • •

My name is Lawrence. I am fifty-seven years old. I am an accountant with the County of Los Angeles. I have three sons, a daughter and two grandchildren. They range in age from five to thirty-five.

There's really not much to tell about my past. I was born and raised in Georgia. After I graduated from high school, I joined the Air Force and did a lot of travelling in Asia and Europe. When I got out, I attended South Carolina State University for two years. Later, I moved to Cleveland where I met my first wife. After a few years, we got tired of the winters so we moved to San Francisco and that's where my kids attended school.

Things were pretty good for us. I worked for several retail stores and eventually got into management. But in 1969, my wife passed. By then the kids were practically grown, so they could pretty much take care of themselves. It took me a while to get over her death. We were very close, but as they say, time heals. Some time later, I remarried. My second wife is a social services administrator and our son is in high school.

• • • • • •

My name is Howard. I am sixty-three years old. I am a retired school teacher. I have a son and a daughter in their thirties.

I was born and raised in a rural area outside Baton Rouge, Louisiana. My father raised chickens and he had a lot of customers, black and white. I left Louisiana to join the Army during World War II.

After I got out of the service, I went back home for a while. I had my GI Bill money, so I enrolled at Dillard University. That's where I met my wife and I'm happy to say that we've been married for nearly forty years. My daughter is married to an attorney in Washington D.C. My son is a draftsman for a company in Virginia.

• • • • • •

My name is Earl Hutchinson, Sr. I am eighty-eight years old. I have a son, daughter, three grandchildren, and two great grandchildren. They range in age from three to fifty-five. In chapter six of this book, my son will tell you my story.

• • • • • •

My name is Earl Ofari Hutchinson. I am forty-six years old. I won't tell you too much about my past and experiences right now. You will learn quite a bit about me as you read *Black Fatherhood*. But I will say this. I have shared many of the same experiences of other fathers and in some cases more.

I have been single, married, separated, divorced and remarried. I have raised a son and a daughter both as a married father and a single father. I have seen the generational changes not only in their lives, but in mine.

# 1

# THE CHALLENGE OF BLACK LIFESTYLES

My father loves to talk about "the good old days." Life, he says, was less complicated then: "We had our share of problems, but we handled them our way." He's right. My father and the black fathers of his day faced bitter discrimination, grinding poverty and family hardship. But they handled these problems their way. They struggled and sacrificed to make a better life for their families. They had their eyes fixed firmly on the future.

While times have changed, black fathers are still handling problems their way. Some of those problems haven't changed. Many African-Americans still face bitter discrimination, poverty and family hardship. Now add to this the tough hurdles of: AIDS, drug addiction, alcoholism, gangs, promiscuous sex and violence, and indeed life can seem like an endless procession of complex and dizzying conflicts and problems.

There is another challenge, perhaps even more perplexing to black men. They must also find a way to break down the barriers of suspicion and distrust between them and their women. Most African-Americans have heard the accusations.

Many black women say black men are: unfaithful, insensitive, exploitive, greedy, selfish and egotistical. In turn, black men say black women are: unfaithful, insensitive, exploitive, greedy, selfish and egotistical. Male-female relationships, including marriage, are an emotional minefield that black fathers must tip lightly through.

HOWARD—*A marriage or a relationship is a partnership. To make it work you have to come to a certain mutual understanding. When problems arise, you first have to create a calm atmosphere to talk. If you can't do that then it won't work. Each one ends up blaming or accusing the other of not doing something or acting a certain way. Then it goes downhill. But if you can create the calm atmosphere where you can really listen to the other person, then you can ask the questions that lead to solutions: Why is this person saying this? Why do they feel this way? What do they want and why do they want it? Is it in my best interest to give ground? Then you have a chance to agree on something that's acceptable to you and your partner.*

Even in the strongest relationships conflicts will arise. Yet conflict is not necessarily bad. If it is handled poorly, it can deepen hostility. If it is handled well, it can deepen understanding. Nowhere is it written that conflict must result in discord or the break up of a relationship. But we must be realistic.

PERRY—*When my girlfriend and I knew that our relationship was serious, we made a joint agreement not to discuss problems without raising possible solutions. There have been a few times when we've had differences over bills, or household functions where either she or I have come close to violating the agreement and getting into a shouting match. But one of us has paused, taken a deep breath, reminded the other that we had an agreement and were about to break it. Either she or I would then ask. 'Is that what you want?' That seems to be enough of a slap to bring the other one back to reality.*

A black father faces special problems that can strain even the healthiest relationships. Often there is not enough money. A child may be doing poorly in school. The streets are dangerous. He is often plagued by the thought that maybe he did not receive a job or promotion because he was black. Some men, said Dr. Martin Luther King. Jr., were defeated by this: "The Negro father became resigned to hopelessness, and he communicated this to his children. Some men unable to communicate the emotional storms struck out at those who would be least likely to destroy them."

Dr. King's life proved that emotional storms need not topple black relationships. They can be overcome.

LAWRENCE—*I've been married more than ten years and I still have conflicts with my wife over things that I thought we had an understanding on. So I've learned that trying to make a relationship work is a twenty-four hour a day job. You have to give when you're not accustomed to giving. You have to almost forget the word "I" and get used to the idea of "us."*

Despite all of his reminiscences, my father knew that some things do not change. Nearly everyone still must buy clothes and food, make rent or mortgage payments, and pay gas, electric and telephone bills. Beyond this, there are the little nagging debts that most people find themselves stuck with. This takes money. Money that is often scarce or nonexistent for many blacks.

Here's why. The gap between black income and white income exceeds one hundred billion dollars; one in three blacks lives below the poverty line; black men consistently have double the rate of unemployment of white males; black families possess only a small fraction of the total wealth of white families. The black poor hover on the brink of permanent depression.

HOWARD—*Some years ago, we had only one car. I had to drive my son and daughter to school and other places and then go to work. My wife had to depend on the bus to go to work and anyplace else she wanted to go. After a while, we were able to save up a little money. I thought that we should pay off some bills that were pressing. My wife disagreed. She wanted to buy a used car.*

*We went back and forth on this for a while. Neither one of us were willing to give in. Finally, she said that she wanted to drive our car and that I should try riding the bus. I said fine. After a couple of days of doing that, I saw that she was right. I hadn't ridden the bus in so long that I forgot the hassle and inconvenience. We bought the car.*

## Saving Their Minds

My eyes were bloodshot. My nerves were on edge. I just wanted to plop down on the sofa and watch TV. I wanted to tune the world out. I had just finished a ten hour stint at my job. But my son held out a book and asked me to read him a story. I groaned silently. This was the last thing I wanted to do that night. I didn't have much choice. It's called quality time and it's the price that fathers must pay for the intellectual and social growth of his children.

ROBERT—*I let my children know that no part of my life was off limits to them. They could ask me whatever they wanted, whenever they wanted. It's surprising how many things you can do that cost little or nothing. I took them to museums, plays, and art exhibits.*

*Even the things I liked to do, I would include them in. When I played basketball, I took them to the playground with me. They might go play or they would watch me. Sometimes, I would drive out to the airport and park the car so they could watch the planes land and take-off.*

*A lot of men think that having their kids with them hampers them or requires a lot of time and effort to watch them or keep up with them. I never really found it a problem. The kids adapted to their surroundings wherever I took them. I found out that kids are a lot more flexible than a lot of adults think.*

There was a time when a man would be offended if anyone called him "house husband" or "Mr. Mom." No more. Many men wear the label as a badge of endearment. To them, it is recognition that they are an equal partner in the nurturing and enrichment of their children.

ROBERT—*My youngest son was six months old when he came to live with me. So I had to do the mothering as well as the fathering. I changed his diapers, fed him, hugged and kissed him. In church, I would sit in the section where the women with babies sat. I had my yellow bag filled with pins, diapers, baby bottles, and pacifiers. I sat there rocking him and nursing him just like the other mothers. I didn't care who looked or said anything. It was something that I had to do and enjoyed doing.*

## GUIDE 1

I include the kids in as many of my activities as possible. It doesn't hamper me or take any extra effort. Kids adapt to their surroundings and will get something out of them.

# Widening the Family Circle

It was a natural thing, even expected. If you needed advice, a dollar or two, help with the kids or a favor you would ask a family member. If family members were unable to help, there were friends to turn to. Nearly every African-American can tell of a warm relationship with an "aunt," "uncle" or "cousin" whom they consider a special member of the family even though they are not related.

The extended family is an ancient and proud tradition among African-Americans. While the storybook family of mom, pop and two kids is American, the extended family is African.

*When you go into a house, first question is, have you had anything to eat? Bring water, you wash and then eat — not one fip you pay. If you are sick nurse you — not one fip you pay. If you want clothing, one woman put in two knots warp, den men weave it, and you cut just such garment you like — not one fip you pay.*

Testimony of an ex-slave, born in the
Gambia River region of West Africa, 1837

The extended family was important in African society because the family, says family expert Andrew

Billingsley, "was an economic and a religious unit which through its ties with wider kinship circles was also a political unit." The key word is "unit." Family members included distant relatives and friends. Mothers and fathers, brothers and sisters, aunts and uncles, grandmothers and grandfathers, nephews and nieces, cousins and close friends. They lived together. They worked together. They shared food and clothes. If there was a special need there was always someone to fulfill it. They had only one motivation: The survival and prosperity of their family. Slavery did not destroy this.

ROBERT—*My uncle, aunt, sister and her husband all helped raise me. I would spend a lot of time at their houses. They would fix food for me and take me places on the weekends. They would go to parties and I would go along with them. They encouraged me in school and they saw to it that I always had a little spending money. Even now, I still can go to them whenever I have a problem. They will help me anyway they can.*

"Uncle Taylor's" visit to our house was a special time for me. You could depend on him showing up at the same time each week. He would spend an hour or two talking or playing checkers with my father or chatting with my mother. He was always good at fixing things. If we had a broken faucet or light socket,

"Uncle" Taylor would repair it. I would hold his tools and he would tell me how important it was for me to "obey my parents," and "to be a good boy."

Before he left, Uncle Taylor would give me a gentle pat on the head and slip me a dollar. He would be sure to say something like "save that money for your schooling." He was a kind and gentle man. He loved us. And even though he was not my real uncle, I loved him, too.

LAWRENCE—*I had a vacant apartment in the building I owned and lived in. I didn't want to rent it out because I thought I might need it for a relative. One of my tenants asked me if I would rent it to one of his relatives. He was a good tenant, so I agreed. As it turned out, the people I rented it to stayed with us for years. They became part of our family. They would buy clothing for my daughter, look after my son. Their door was always open to us. We thought nothing of going up and eating with them or borrowing something from them. It was the same on my end. Whatever I could do for them, I did.*

## Is "Women's Work" Only for Women?

Is there such a thing as "women's work?" Once many people thought so. Each day, the husband marched off to his office or factory job while his wife cleaned, cooked and took care of the kids. At the end of the day the husband returned home, settled in his easy chair, read the paper or watched TV. His wife dutifully greeted him with a smile and a kiss. There was always a hot meal waiting. He would have been indignant if she had asked him to help her with the housework.

PERRY—*I cook at least three days each week. It was a chore at first but after a while it was fun trying out new things. If I go to a restaurant and I see a dish that looks interesting, and that I think my kids would enjoy. I try to find out the ingredients and fix it. It's always a surprise for the kids. I experiment with all kinds of combinations. I try to make sure that I have the right balance—vegetables, breads, fish and chicken.*

In many black households things worked this way because black women usually worked. Their pay-checks were needed to pay the bills. The husband and wife more or less worked as a team to beat back hard times. The black woman did not have the luxury of playing the perfect little housewife.

This had far reaching implications. If the wife had to work outside the home, then it was only fair that men should work inside the home. Many did. With four out of five black women working, many more will have to.

LAWRENCE—*I figure that by helping my wife with the housework. I am making things more comfortable for her. And if I make things more comfortable for her, I make them more comfortable for me.*

If my father considered cooking, cleaning and ironing "women's work," he hid his feelings well. He didn't complain when my mother occasionally asked him to help her. Later, when she was briefly hospitalized, my father became the breadwinner and apron wearer. That's when the fun began. More than once, I sat at the table and stared at the burnt rice on my plate. My shirts that he starched often felt like a medieval torture mask.

## GUIDE 2

I figure that by helping my wife with the housework. I am making things more comfortable for her—and me.

One rule my father had wasn't as much fun. If my sister had to cook, clean and iron so did I. In later years, these skills came in handy. Often my first wife left so early for work that she did not have enough time to wash and iron. So I did. She would come in late from work too tired to cook and clean. So I did. Those were the times when I thanked him for teaching me "women's work."

## Being Better Than "They" Are

"I want you to be better than "they are." My father's words puzzled me. Later I found out who the "they" were. When black fathers tell their children that they have to be better than white people to get ahead they are pointing out the sad reality of America. They know that blacks are more likely to be judged on the color of their skin than the content of their character. They know that they must be prepared to be the best they can in any trade or profession they choose.

PERRY—*One day my daughter came home from pre-school in tears. I asked her what was wrong. She said that some white kids had called her ugly because she was black. I told her that she was a very pretty little girl and that color doesn't make a person ugly. I told her that there are some people who will try to tell her that she's no good because she is black, but she must never believe them. I pointed out to her that there were blacks on TV and in magazines. And no one could say they were ugly.*

*We went over the physical features of her black Barbie doll— nose, eyes, lips, hair, and ears. I asked her if she thought they were any uglier than her white Barbies. She said no. After that, I watched to make sure that she played with both of them equally. She did.*

A. Phillip Randolph enjoyed many satisfying moments during his long and great career as a fighter for labor equity, justice and human rights. But there was always one which gave him special satisfaction. As a boy in Jacksonville, Florida, Randolph fondly remembered that his father forbade him to set foot in the city's main library, or spend a penny to ride the street cars. They were segregated. The Reverend James Randolph would not allow his son to cooperate with injustice. Randolph never did.

ROBERT—*I tell my sons that your appearance and the way you act are important. Many people judge you on that. I want them to leave the house neat and clean. Also, I teach my sons to look everyone they talk with directly in the eye. I tell them to hold their head erect, speak confidently and with a strong voice. Sometimes this causes problems for them with some whites. They seem to expect blacks to act shy or withdrawn. If they don't, they take it as a sign of defiance or aggressiveness. But I feel that in the long run a person who is confident and secure about himself will go much further.*

## Taming the Mean Streets

"If Martin Luther King, Jr. and Malcolm X were

> ## GUIDE 3
>
> I teach my sons to look everyone they talk with directly in the eye. I tell them to hold their heads erect, speak confidently and with a strong voice.

alive they would hang their head in shame at us." The ex-gang member is right. Between 1980 and 1985, 44,428 black males were murdered in the United States. Let's put the number in better perspective. The death toll exceeds the number of American soldiers killed in Korea (34,000), and nearly equals the number of American soldiers killed in Vietnam (47,000). If the killing pace continues, by the close of the first decade of the 21st Century, it will surpass the number of American soldiers killed during World War II (292,000).

Behind each of these numbers, there is the personal pain and agony that family members and loved ones suffer. The newspapers don't talk about that, but it's there.

ROBERT—*I keep a constant look out for changes in my son's behavior. I watch how he dresses. Has he started wearing his pants low? Does he wear caps, jackets? I pay*

*close attention to who is calling the house. If I hear a name
mentioned that I am not familiar with, I ask him about that
person. When he goes out, I take note of what time he comes
home. The big thing is school. Is he keeping up his grades? Is
he getting to school on time, or at all? Whenever I can, I
escort him to activities he's involved with.*

I wasn't eavesdropping, but Milton said something
to my son that caught my attention. Milton was my
son's friend and high school classmate. They were
talking about a close call they had in the neighborhood.
I asked Milton to tell me what happened.

At first, he was reluctant to talk and my son was
silent. So I kept at them. Finally, Milton told me that
some gang members had shaken them down for money
on their way home from school. Fortunately, Milton
knew one of the boys faintly. It was just enough to save
them both from a beating or worse.

Later, I questioned my son closely about it. I could
tell that it was something that he'd prefer to let drop.
He was adhering to the traditional teen code of silence
that parents know well. It's their way of exerting
independence. Their silence says, "I can make my own
decisions and handle my own problems." Maybe.

Still, I felt it was important for my son to realize the

danger of gangs. After much discussion, he reluctantly told me where it happened. A few days later, I made a discreet call to a friend at City Hall who had contacts with programs that work with gang members. I knew he would follow up. Although I never spoke of the incident again, the fear was there.

ROBERT—*My son likes to wear caps and jackets. This has tended to be associated with gang attire. I don't panic and accuse him of involvement with gangs. A lot of kids like to wear caps and jackets. They think it's cool. It's their way of identifying. But it doesn't mean that they belong to any gangs. With my son, I started early. I made sure that he was involved in a variety of sports and after school activities. He had full exposure to activities that kept him out of the street. This is really important. If you don't start early with them, by the time they hit the teen years, they are vulnerable to the bad elements out there in the streets.*

It seems that black fathers spend many waking hours fighting to prevent their children from becoming grim statistics. That was true for my father. Years after I graduated from college and married, my father told me "You never knew how many nights that your mother and I stayed awake worrying about you when you were out." They breathed easier only after they heard the door close behind me when I came home.

Many black fathers know what he is talking about. They live in constant dread that they will receive a late night call from the police telling them that their son or daughter has been injured, assaulted or jailed. When it involves their children's safety, sleep is a commodity that will always be in short supply.

PERRY—*Before I enrolled my daughter in the school she attends, I drove through the neighborhood several times before and after school. I wanted to see what the kids looked like who went to the school. I looked at how they dressed and how they acted. I parked across from the school to see if there were kids that were hanging around that weren't students. Once when I picked her up I saw some kids who looked like they didn't belong there. I called the principal to let her know that there might be a problem.*

They comfort. They nurture. They understand their problems. They satisfy their needs. They provide refuge from a world that seems hostile and uncaring. I'm talking about gangs. They have been with us for decades. Many young people join them to validate their existence and reinforce their fragile egos. But gangs also kill, injure and maim. They deal in guns and drugs. They disrupt the community and deepen the fears of many African-Americans. Gangs are stamped with a permanent warning: Join at your own risk.

## Chasing the 'White Lady'

"If anyone had asked me around the latter part of 1957 just what I thought had made the greatest impression on my generation in Harlem, I would have said 'Drugs'." Novelist Claude Brown is close. Except I would not use the word "impression." Drugs have been a deadly curse on a generation of African-Americans.

LAWRENCE—*When I talk to my son about drugs, I try to use examples that he can relate too. I might tell him about a baseball or basketball player who had a multi-million dollar contract and screwed up because he couldn't get a handle on his drug habit. This seems to get his attention. I think this is better than preaching to him.*

The mural of Uncle Sam painted on an Oakland grocery store was captioned, "Uncle Crack." It depicted America's crowning symbol of Democracy pushing a long line of naked and chained blacks to a door marked suicide. At one time, drugs were a haven from the pain and oppression of life for a few street corner junkies. Now they are everyone's universal nightmare. Their deadly tentacles have reached out and ensnared thousands of black households. Nearly everyone has a hard luck story to tell of a friend or relative who has been involved with drugs. Many have attended funerals of those who died from overdoses or were killed in a drug battle or after a deal went sour.

ROBERT—*There were times I smoked dope when I was young. It was hard not too. The stuff was everywhere. Parties, school, even at the playground where I played basketball. Guys would be puffing or snorting between games. You couldn't avoid it. So I know the dangers of drugs and I tell my son about my experiences. I let him know that they didn't help me in my studies, put money in my pocket, or make me a better person. I think he may have gotten the message. A couple of times at school he was approached and asked to sell dope. He refused. How do I know? He told me.*

They called him "Big Red." He made his living on the streets of Harlem as a pimp, hustler, robber, but he made his biggest scores selling drugs. Like most petty criminals, his time on the streets was short-lived. He was arrested and sent to prison. There he read. He

## GUIDE 4

I talk to my son about drugs and use examples he can relate to. I might tell him about a baseball or basketball player who had a multi-million dollar contract and screwed up because of drug use.

studied. He joined the Nation of Islam. He found redemption. "Big Red" became Malcolm X.

As his fame and popularity grew, he never forgot his experience on the streets. It was a lesson and a warning for others. Malcolm knew that the fight against the drug plague would be Herculean. He believed that most drug addicts were, "trying to narcotize themselves against being a black man in the white man's America."

Malcolm saw the damage drugs wreaked among African-Americans. He eagerly jumped into the fray to wipe them out. He had to. He was more than a political leader; he was a father with four daughters that he loved deeply. His program for "salvaging" young blacks from addiction became a model of success. Malcolm kept the faith.

PERRY—*Sometimes when I'm out and the kids are with me, I drive down a street where I know that drugs are being sold. I point out the dealers to them. I want them to see what they look like. I want them to see what drugs are doing to them. I don't make judgments about them as people. I don't get into the rightness or wrongness of their lives. I think it's more important for the kids to see how drugs can harm a person mentally and physically. Maybe, this will be enough to make them have a revulsion to drugs.*

Drive through any black neighborhood, and what do you see advertised on the billboards and bus stops? What are the main products sold in the stores there? Alcohol and tobacco. They do not get the publicity of hard drugs. They are not part of major national campaigns or crusades. They do not spread panic in communities.

Yet alcohol and tobacco are far more deadly to African-Americans. Each year they claim more black lives than hard drugs.

When America's liquor bill is totaled, blacks will pay more than twelve billion dollars. They will buy nearly one-third of the Scotch Whiskey sold in the country. One in five blacks is alcohol addicted. Three out of five young blacks drink.

If they drink, they are likely to smoke. African-Americans will buy triple the number of cigarettes that whites buy. They are twice as likely to die from lung cancer, emphysema and other respiratory ailments as whites. At least hard drugs are illegal; alcohol and tobacco aren't.

HOWARD—*I practice what I preach. I don't drink or smoke. I don't keep alcohol in my house. I have a sign on my front door that reads, 'Smoking Not Allowed Inside.' When friends visit that smoke, they go outside or they wait until they leave before smoking. If my son saw me drinking and smoking, then I wouldn't have much credibility if I told him not to do it.*

My father dropped the phone and rushed from the house. He was on his way to the police station. They told him that his brother had been arrested and charged with manslaughter in the traffic deaths of two pedestrians. It was no secret in the family that Uncle James had a severe drinking problem. He was an alcoholic.

More than once, before this, he had gotten into minor scrapes after a prolonged bout with the bottle. Often my father would give him a few dollars to help him out of a problem, but this was the worst. My father would spend hours in court and pay a small fortune in attorney fees to get my uncle released. Later a settlement was quietly made with the relatives of the victims.

But Uncle James did not stop drinking. A few years later they found him dead in the bathtub. Apparently, he had fallen and hit his head. By then he was living out of his suitcase at a tiny neighborhood hotel. His death was ruled an accident. He had been drinking.

My father always felt obliged to help him. It cost him money. It caused him pain. How many other Uncle James' are there?

ROBERT—*I used to keep a couple of bottles of Scotch around the house for guests. When I got home one evening I saw one of the bottles sitting on the kitchen table with the top off. There was a glass in the sink with some drops of alcohol in it. My son was the only other person in the house at the time. I immediately threw the bottles in the trash and I have not had another bottle of liquor in the house since.*

Racism. Poverty. Gangs. Drugs. Family Roles. Male-Female Relationships. These problems seem more complicated and demanding than ever. So my father was right. Nothing is simple anymore. The only thing that has not changed is that black fathers must still confront those problems, as my father would say, their way.

# 2

# Don't Leave Education to the Schools!

I found out the hard way the truth of the old adage that education is too important to be left to the schools. I remember the sinking feeling I got during a parent conference I had with my son's algebra teacher. He told me that my son had not attended a single class in the last month. It must be a mistake, I weakly protested. I had taken great care each morning to see that he arrived at school on time. I sometimes lingered an extra moment and watched as he disappeared into the school entrance.

I just knew that my son was doing well in his studies. And now to hear the teacher tell me this abruptly shattered my illusions—or maybe delusions. The only thing the teacher was wrong about was the time. My son had gone, not a month, but nearly the entire semester without attending a single class. As the teacher and I spoke, my son sat at his desk staring out the window. He did not look at either of us. I told him we would have a long talk when he got home.

I got home early that evening. I was anxious to get to the bottom of this. My son was not there. Several hours passed and it grew darker. I called the police. Even though he hadn't been gone long enough to be considered a runaway, they said they would keep a look out for him in the neighborhood.

After a few calls, I found him at the house of one of his friends. He was ashamed, embarrassed, but mostly scared. Why did he skip class? Rather than admit that he didn't understand the lessons, he simply "got lost" on the playground every day.

Should I blame his teacher for not taking enough interest in my son to find out the reason for his absence? Of course. Should I blame his counselor for not following-up to see that he was not having difficulties with the class? Of course. Should I blame the administration for not making sure that both did their jobs? Of course.

Should I blame myself for not doing my job at home? Of course.

Many black fathers have learned the bitter lesson that when it comes to their child's education: Take nothing for granted.

PERRY—*I try to think up different ways to participate directly with my daughter in her education. When we're in the car, we may sing the ABCs. If we stop for a passing train, we'll count the cars as they go by. I buy a lot of mix and match picture and word books and we work them together. When we read a storybook, I read one page and she reads another. When we finish, we make up little quizzes about the story and we test each other. I figure that if she sees that I'm interested in what she's doing, then she can't help but be interested too.*

For decades, most blacks were educated in segregated rural schools and black colleges. They were desperately poor and the facilities were substandard. The teachers and administrators did the best with what they had. They were tough. They were proud.

They cared. And because they did, some worked minor miracles because they wanted their students to excel. Many did.

That has changed. For many black children the educational deck is so badly stacked against them today that they are branded "at risk." Only one in ten black children attend private school. Many of the public schools are dangerous, poorly funded, overcrowded, badly staffed with inexperienced teachers and run by insensitive administrators.

One in two students will be robbed or assaulted. Nearly one out of two black students leave school as a functional illiterate. Their SAT test scores drag the bottom of the scale. Only three in ten will ever reach college.

LAWRENCE—*Books. Books. Books. I keep them in the kitchen, bathroom, living room and everywhere else in the house. When I take my son shopping, if there's a bookstore close by, I make it a point to stop in. I may not buy anything, but we'll spend time just browsing.*

Many who do stay in school don't share the fate of the one out of four black youths who drop out. The doors of opportunity slam tight against those who drop out; so tight that one out of two of them earn no income for their families. They must fend for themselves on the cruel and hostile streets of the ghetto. Many drift through a world of low paid, dead end jobs, or fall into the pit of hustling, petty crime, or drug dealing. This path often leads to only two places: death or prison.

ROBERT—*I try to provide an atmosphere for my three sons that's conducive to studying and doing homework. I have three desks and two table tops in the house. They can always find a quiet place to work. When they're working, I don't look over their shoulders to see what they're doing. But I make sure I am at home during their study time so that if they have any questions they can ask.*

"At risk" black children are the victims of an educational system close to shambles and almost everyone concerned seems to have a plan for repairing the damage.

They call for: more enrichment programs, remedial reading, ungraded classrooms, team or mentor teaching. Some even turn to desperate solutions such as all-black schools, separate classrooms and boot camp academies.

Many of them say, "give us more money and we will solve the problem." But money or high gloss programs alone won't solve the problem. There are no mysteries to educational success.

LAWRENCE—*I enrolled my son in an after school workshop. They learn about black and African history and culture. They are very strong on discipline. They emphasize doing your work and finishing it on time. Each month, the students are assigned projects to complete and they are given a deadline. They can work individually or as a team. My son chose to do a research paper on Frederick Douglass and how he fought against slavery. He read several books on Douglass. He collected some pictures of him and he interviewed a black writer who had done some work on Douglass. He did all the work himself and he finished it before the due date.*

Here's what black fathers can do to ensure educational success. They can work as individuals or form father committees to work with teachers and administrators to plan activities, conferences, events for parents and students. They can volunteer to work as a classroom assistant, tutor or aide. They can organize father advisory councils to advise school administrators on policy, programs and philosophy for their children's education. They can join and work actively in PTAs, Parent Advisory and School Site Councils. They can attend school board meetings and voice their concerns.

They can accept nothing less for their children than an orderly environment free of disciplinary problems and vandalism, high academic expectations, concise, clear instructional objectives and a congenial learning climate conducive for maximum achievement. When they succeed, they can claim credit. When they fail they must accept blame.

HOWARD —*I didn't wait for parent conferences to talk with my son or daughter's teachers. Each month, I met with every one of them. I checked the papers that she had turned in. I looked at the books they assigned them and questioned them about the chapters or lessons they were doing. I asked the teachers for a copy of the work they assigned their class for the month. If they didn't have it written down, I wrote it down myself. When report cards were due, they did not send them home through the mail or give it to my son and daughter. I picked them up personally. This gave me another opportunity to talk to the teachers and trouble shoot if there were problems.*

If all else fails, they can even do what one father did. Tired of hearing  excuses from his son and teachers why his son received poor grades, he literally went back to school. Every day he and his son sat in class together. They did the classwork together. They checked the home work assignments together. They took the tests together. His son graduated with honors.

HOWARD—*If teachers feel that parents don't care then why should they?*

Many black fathers have stood on the sidelines and turned the task of educating their children over to black women. Some did this because they were indifferent or felt inadequate educationally. Others, battered and buffeted by the struggle for survival, abandoned hope. But many didn't get involved simply because they believed that education, like child rearing, was a chore that should fall on the shoulders of women.

Black mothers certainly deserve praise for their efforts. Many overcame horrendous obstacles and did a masterful job in sustaining their children's intellectual growth. Black fathers, however, have nurturing and bonding skills, too. They are essential for the total development of black youth. If those skills aren't used, it's like putting a picture that's half painted on the wall. It's a picture, but everyone can see that something is missing.

ROBERT —*I paint a picture of life for my sons. I tell them that the life that you make for yourself is the life that you're going to have to live. You can work hard, apply yourself in school and be a success. You can do the minimum, or nothing in school; and be a failure. The choice is yours.*

Black fathers must be motivators and initiators. They can follow the trail blazed by generations of brilliant educators; men who directed black colleges and universities-Atlanta University, Tuskegee, Fisk, Morehouse, Spellman, Morris-Brown, Dillard, Alcorn A&M, Southern University, Orangeburg, Texas Southern, Hampton Institute, and dozens more.

Black educators were guided by a grand vision for their youth. They did not accept the racist myths and stereotypes of black inferiority. They were single-minded in their mission to show that blacks if given a chance could attain the highest levels in society.

## GUIDE 5

I try to think up different ways to participate directly with my daughter in her education. When we're in the car, we may sing the ABCs. If we get stopped for a passing train, we'll count the cars as they go by.

## Sports: Ticket Out of the Ghetto?

Sports sociologist Harry Edwards once said that a high school athlete will get hit on the head by a meteorite before he will make a professional sports team. Odds makers agree with Edwards. They put the average high school football or basketball player's chances at signing a professional contract at one in 18,000. In other words, for every Magic Johnson or Michael Jordan that signs a multi-million dollar contract there are thousands more who won't.

Yet young blacks still spend countless hours dreaming of the big payday that superstardom will surely bring. We see them everyday. They pack the gyms. They fill up the baseball diamonds. They jam the football fields. They sweat and toil for years trying to be a future star on the basketball court or the football field. Their heads swim with visions of money and glory.

But reality has a harsh way of intruding on even the most pleasant of dreams. Many of the 17,999 black athletes who do not receive a professional contract will wind up their sports years with no degree, no training, and, in many cases, no job. They won't have the foggiest notion of what to do with their lives. Is the dream they so feverishly pursue worth it? If the price is more educational waste and the risk is spawning another generation of educational cripples, the answer is no.

ROBERT—*The first year my son went out for the football team his grades stayed reasonably good. By his second year, he had moved up to become the starting halfback on the team.*

*That's when I began to notice a change. He was getting home later and later from school. He seemed more distracted when we talked. The only thing he seemed interested in reading was the sports section.*

*I can't say I was surprised when his report card showed that he received Ds in Algebra and English. First, I talked with his coaches and they started to tell me how good a player he was and all that. I made it clear that I was more interested in how good a student he was. I told them, and then I told my son, that if his grades didn't improve, he would be an-ex member of their team. They got the message.*

It didn't matter to me whether the warning about the futility of a sports career came from Edwards or my father. The coaches told me that I was valuable to my high school football team and that was enough. I dreamt of making the big play that turned the game around. My ears rang with the cheers from the crowd. It was too exhilarating. Books, tests, homework, study? That wasn't for me.

When my father asked me how I did in school, I had ready answers, "Oh, just fine." When he asked, "Where are your books?" My answer, "I don't need them. We're not having any tests and the teacher hasn't given us any assignments lately anyway." After working sometimes nine and ten hours at the Post Office, I figured he was too tired to go to my school to check. I couldn't tell him what I really thought—school meant nothing, sports everything.

PERRY—*Sports is my first love. So I don't encourage or discourage my kids from participating. I tell them that when they run, count the steps, sing a song, or recite the ABCs.*

Black Fathers must continually ask themselves:

• Is it as important to have another fullback in the household as it is to have a dentist, a lawyer, or a plumber?

• Will another football quarterback or basketball forward enhance the cultural and social development of African-Americans?

• Should young blacks spend countless hours trying to master ball handling at the expense of mastering economics, law, medicine, computer science, or a trade?

HOWARD—*I think that sports is an excellent outlet for kids. But they should play not for the benefit of the coaches, since all they care about is winning, rather they should play for themselves. It should be enjoyable. At the same time, I repeat over and over to my son that I am going to check your*

*homework and make sure you are doing your assignments.*
*I don't leave that up to the coaches or the teachers. It's not*
*their responsibility, it's mine.*

Now don't get me wrong. I love sports. I love to
watch the ballet-like moves of professional basketball
players. I delight at the speed and power of great
football running backs. The black athlete has been a joy
and an inspiration to generations of Americans—Jessie
Owens, Josh Gibson, Jackie Robinson, Willie Mays,
Hank Aaron, Jim Brown, Gale Sayers, Tank Younger,
Wilt Chamberlain, Bill Russell, Magic Johnson, Joe
Louis, Sugar Ray Robinson and Muhammad Ali. Their
accomplishments will forever grace the sports annals
of America. Yes, sports has kept more than one young
black off the streets and in school.

LAWRENCE—*If a kid is able to get on a sports team, I think*
*that is good. It teaches them discipline and the importance of*
*working with others. This is their first taste of being a part*
*of an organization. This can be an advantage later on in life.*
*They will be working for a company. Or they may start their*
*own business. Either way, they will need to be disciplined to*
*be successful.*

Through high school and my first year of college, I
spent hours on the practice field trying to learn my
football blocking assignments. I wanted to be the best

at all costs. Books continued to be a vague after-thought. Then my bubble burst. I was injured. The same coaches who praised me when I nearly broke my neck for them on the field suddenly were too busy for me. I was placed on academic probation at the end of my first year. My father didn't give up. We talked and talked some more. He put it directly to me. Did I want to wind up as a faceless, nameless statistic on the streets? Did I want to become another monument to ghetto failure? In time we turned it around, but it was a struggle.

PERRY—*My son is pretty big. When people look at him they say, 'He looks like a football player.' I say no, he looks like the agent for a football player. The football player takes the beating, the agent gets a percentage of his earnings for representing him. By saying this, I try to get my son to see that there are alternatives to sports even within sports. He can use his intelligence and skills to make just as much money without the risks or disappointments.*

## What Do You Want to be When You Grow Up?

If a list was made of the most frequently asked questions, it would probably rank near the top: "What do you want to be when you grow up?" Most black fathers ask their son or daughter the question. Parents are anxious about their children's future. Many black fathers look at their lives. They see it as a struggle. They want their children to be "something better" than they were.

LAWRENCE—*Most children say they want to be a fireman or police officer. Why? Those are the persons that they see most often on the street and on TV. They are glamorized. What I try to do is to expose my children to other kinds of professions. I talk with them about the skills required to be a doctor, lawyer, bank manager, building contractor, businessperson, plumber and just about any other occupation I feel is productive.*

*When I worked as a manager at a department store, I would often take my son and daughter with me to the store. They didn't really do any work. I just wanted them to be there so they could see how a store is run from the inside. I wanted them to know it's more important to have a career than just a job.*

Despite school desegregation, increased college opportunities and affirmative action, America's promise of equal opportunity for many African-Americans remains just that—a promise. One out of three blacks is employed in an unskilled or semi-skilled job.

While more African-Americans moved into skilled occupations, the top of the managerial and professional pyramid is white and male. As the occupation goes, so goes the income. The result: for every dollar white males make, blacks make about sixty cents. Black Fathers ask: How long will my son's or daughter's income remain a fraction of somebody else's?

LAWRENCE—*I don't tell my son what I think he should be or what I want him to be. He will have to make that choice for himself. I do make sure that he is taking the courses in school that will properly prepare him for a career. If he is, then he can go in any direction that he wants to go.*

Through slavery and segregation, Black fathers clung tightly to the promise and hope of education. They believed that this could "lift the yoke" of poverty and despair from their lives and those of their children. Despite the odds, that hope remains unchanged.

## GUIDE 6

I make sure my son is taking the courses in school that will prepare him for a career. If he is, then he can go in any direction that he wants to go.

# 3

# SEX, HEALTH AND OURSELVES

America has long been fascinated with black men. Much of their fascination is a product of the mythology from slavery. The slave masters believed that black men played fast and loose with the rules of morality. They were studs, super-sexed, lustful and coarse. They were cruel and abusive toward their women and children. They cared very little about their health and the quality of their lives.

The mythology later was used as one of the excuses to maintain segregation. It still causes problems for black men.

PERRY—My *daughter who is six-years-old told me that she knew how mommy got pregnant. Her explanation was that she eats food and the crumbs pile up in her stomach and make a baby. I said no, that's not how it happened. I told her that I love her mother very much. I said when two people love each other, one of the ways that they express that love is through physical relations.*

*I told her that men and women have different body parts and explained how they are used. I used a children's manual on the human anatomy that my doctor had recommended. It described the reproductive process in lay terms. It was easy for her to follow and for me to explain.*

It's tempting to say that blacks are uninformed or irresponsible in their sex and health practices. Therefore, they have higher rates of teenage pregnancy, infant mortality, disease and early death. The main problem is not lack of information but lack of access to quality, affordable health care. Information, however, is still very important to live a safe and healthy life. And one of the greatest gifts black fathers can give their children is information. It starts with the basics. They must talk to their children truthfully and honestly about sex.

LAWRENCE—*It's not easy for adults to talk openly with their children about sex. I know I found myself stammering when my son, who was ten-years-old at the time, asked me a question about women. I fumbled for the right words. I wasn't sure exactly what to say. I didn't want to say the wrong thing. It turned out my son had a health class where they talked about the human body and its functions. My son already knew quite a bit. That broke the ice. I felt more comfortable talking with him about the sex act, pregnancy and the importance of health and hygiene.*

My father said it. I'm sure his father said it. His father before him and so on. Any man can make a baby, but only a father can raise a baby. Many black fathers do all they can to shield their children from health and sexual dangers. Even so, far too many young black males are making babies.

A black teen is four times more likely to give birth than a white teen. The child that has a child bears the burden of feeding, clothing and caring for the baby. And what if the father is in a gang or in jail? Who provides the support? Will the mother return to school? Probably not. So what kind of future can she hope for? Young women ask the father: Isn't this your son or daughter, too? Young men must ask themselves: Am I a man or a father? There's a difference.

ROBERT—*My son is twelve-years-old. I've had several talks with him about sex. I tell him that the Christian way is not to have sex before marriage. But I'm not naive. I know that my son has eyes and ears. He can see that this isn't the way the world is. So I also make it clear that when people engage in sex who aren't married they should always use a condom or some other form of protection.*

*I explain the risks and the types of diseases that can be contracted. But the biggest thing that I stress is responsibility. If you make a baby, you are going to have to take care of it. It's not just up to the girl. I asked him, 'You say you want to be an engineer, do you think you can finish school, go on to college, and complete your studies taking care of a baby AND its mother too?' He is always silent.*

Some young, unmarried black fathers try to do the right thing. But they frequently are on shaky financial ground. Only one in four will be able to support their family above the poverty level. Seven out of ten black children in single mother households are poor. It's frightening to think that we continue to lose the flower of our youth to the dustbin of neglect.

HOWARD—*I didn't believe in preaching or scolding my daughter when it came to sex. I didn't believe trying to scare them was a good way to get your message across. I tried to use reason and appealed to her intelligence and common sense. She knew about the problems of disease. She saw some of her high school classmates that dropped out of school because they got pregnant. So she was receptive to hearing the facts.*

My father would tell my sister to keep her dress down and her pants up. It was a caustic warning that fathers have always given their daughters. For some reason, I can't remember him telling me to keep my pants zipped up. When it comes to sex education there is clearly a double standard. Many men are like the proverbial gunfighter of the Old West who notched his gun with every kill. They measure theur manhood by how many sexual conquests they've had. If fathers wink and nod at their son's sexual follies, they send the message that adventure, not caution, is the watch-word.

They also perpetuate the ritual. It goes like this. Young men get together and brag about their romantic escapades. One tries to top the other. The juicier the story the better. It's mostly puffery and everybody knows it. But that's OK, it's part of the game that make boys men. Or is it?

ROBERT—*Sometimes I hear my son talking on the phone with his friends. Kids talk different with each other. They use different language that adults don't hear or understand.*

*They have a whole different personality. He tries to sound wise and worldly. But I laugh. To hear him tell it, he has a different girl every night. But that's pretty hard especially when every night I know he stays closed up in his room most of the time.*

*But I don't completely ignore him when I hear him use certain words or say things that are out of line. I call him on it. I ask him if he knows that these words not only are unflattering to girls, but don't make him any more of a man. I tell him to look closely at the men who women most admire and watch how they act. They are gentlemen. And this is what attracts most women to men.*

---

**GUIDE 7**

I make it clear to my son that when people who aren't married engage in sex they should use a condom. If something happens and you make a baby you are going to have to take care of it.

---

## When Health is More Than Wealth

Many Americans were shocked to learn that black men in Harlem have a lower life expectancy than men in Bangladesh, one of the world's poorest countries. Most African-Americans weren't. They know that America's health chart for them is poor or non-existent.

Black infants are twice as likely to die as white infants. This happens not because blacks are by nature more sickly, but because black babies are three times more likely to have a lower birth weight than whites. Chalk that up to poverty, lack of pre-natal care and poor nutrition.

ROBERT—*As my sons have gotten older, I've become much more health conscious. I don't smoke. As for drinking, I may have an occasional beer or glass of wine but that's about it. We eat three meals a day. There's always bread, fruit and juices around the house for them to snack on. I try to cut down on eating at fast food places. But sometimes, you can't help it.*

*When we go, I make sure that we get a salad and either low fat milk or fruit juice.*

The chances of blacks dying from the big killers— cancer, heart disease, stroke diabetes and infectious diseases—are much greater than for whites. This happens because blacks have less opportunity to see a doctor, less access to hospitals, less insurance and less money to pay for any of this.

There's more. Blacks die in greater numbers because they don't have proper information about medical treatment, services, diet and nutrition. Prevention can only come with information. Without it, the battle against discrimination and injustice will be harder for blacks to win because too many will be lost to sickness and death.

PERRY—*I make sure my son and daughter have annual check-ups. I keep their immunizations current. When they leave the house, if it's cold they wear a jacket and a hat. I check their bedroom at night to make sure the windows are closed, there are blankets on the bed and they are wearing pajamas. I took them to a health fair that my church sponsored. I picked up a lot of literature on disease prevention. A lot of the stuff was geared toward children. I went over it with them.*

The pain on the face of the man standing in front of his church talking to a friend told of a father's agony. Ervin Johnson, Sr. was trying to come to grips with the fact that his son had tested HIV positive. He was a father who knew that his son, Magic Johnson, could die from AIDS.

HOWARD—*How long does it take to put a condom on? Or better yet, how long does it take to say no?*

Ervin Johnson, Sr. was not alone. Many other black

fathers must face the grim reality that their son or daughter may die of AIDS. One in three Americans who die of AIDS is black. One out of two children under thirteen years of age with AIDS is black.

Before 1988, Americans had never heard of the term "boarder baby." They have now because hospitals throughout the country must care for them. They are babies who are infected with HIV. They received it from their mothers. Most of them are black.

PERRY—*Several times during the year, they hold a health awareness week at my daughter's school. They pick a different topic and spend a day or so on it. It might be hypertension, AIDS, cancer, or nutrition. I have volunteered to help with the displays and the information tables. It's good for the kids but it also gives me a chance to stay informed about diseases and their effects on African-Americans. I'm always amazed at how much free information there is out there. I think it's up to us to take advantage of it.*

During a visit to my grandmother in the small farmtown of Clarksville, Missouri, I came down with polio. When they notified my father, he didn't hesitate. He took the first train to St. Joseph where I was hospitalized. The day after his arrival he had me transferred from the aging hospital to a larger, better equipped facility in St. Louis. He wasn't taking any chances. The type of polio I had was mild and treatable. When I was released several weeks later, my father was there to take me home.

---

**GUIDE 8**

I've become much more health conscious. I don't smoke. I rarely drink and I keep bread, fruit and juices around the house for my kids to snack on.

---

## Respect Yourself

"Bitch," "Nig," "Fag," "Ho," "Slut," "Dude," "Stuff," "Dog," "Piece." Is this what black boys think of black girls? Is this what black girls think of black boys? If some do, then we've strayed badly.

There was a time in the not too distant past when poet Paul Laurence Dunbar proudly told the world in his *Negro Love Song* that the black woman was his "honey." The gleam in her eye and her radiant beauty was so intense that he had to "jump back." There was nothing he wouldn't do for her. He spoke for many black men in those days.

Some years later civil rights leader, Fannie Lou Hamer would tell the world that her husband was six foot three, two hundred and forty pounds and wore a size 14 shoe. She was not ashamed to say that she loved every square inch of him. And in case somebody missed her point, she quickly added that she was not about to "liberate" herself from him.

HOWARD—*Back then our words to each other seemed to mean more than they do today. When we said 'I do' to the preacher, it meant just that, 'I do.'*

It's sad to hear the words: "You know a Nig . . . ain't s . . . ." These words have become so much a part of their vocabulary of denial and self-hate that many blacks say them without a second thought. Only someone totally blind to the realities of life would say that black men are completely blameless. They aren't putty-like victims misshaped by an unjust social system.

Many have shirked their responsibilities toward their wives and children. Many have shown by their actions and words that they do have profound contempt for the black women who have loved them. Many others view women as sex objects, playthings to be used and discarded like so many broken toys.

These men do not deserve praise. They do not

deserve excuses. When relationships between black men and black women are firmly structured on the twin pillars of trust and mutual respect, they can withstand the daily shocks of poverty, racism, personal insults and emotional tension. But if one or the other pillars is shaken, the structure will fall.

HOWARD—*Maybe I'm old fashioned, but I don't see anything wrong with going out of your way to offer a woman a seat or to open the door for her. I think it is very appropriate to give ladies flowers or cards on occasions. To me, these are expressions that show that men care about women. I don't believe that women object to receiving them.*

I was apprehensive. My daughter had a boyfriend. It was her first real romantic involvement. The warning signals went up. I was a boy myself and I remembered what I often thought about girls. It wasn't always flattering. I tried to put her romance in perspective. Sooner or later it was bound to happen. It was hard but I had to trust her.

On Peter's first visit to the house, I tried not to subject him to the Spanish Inquisition. I casually asked him about school, his parents and his interests. I tried to do most of the listening.

PERRY—*I want my daughter to get to know different men.*

*This doesn't mean going to bed with them or having affairs with them. I mean get to know them as individuals, as friends—their interests, hobbies, their likes and dislikes. I don't want her to be inhibited around them. I want her to talk with them about political and social issues. I want them to see that she has a mind, too. And I want her to see that there are many men who are thoughtful and considerate. Not all of them want only one thing from a woman.*

The second time Peter visited, I focused on my daughter. I told him about her school, tennis, music and friends. This time he did most of the listening. On a subsequent visit, I talked with him with my daughter present. I explored his feelings about her—not as a girl-friend, but as a person. This was important. I felt if he respected her as a person, he would respect her as a young woman. I wanted her to hear what he had to say. It was part of her education in the ways of men.

LAWRENCE—*I tell my son that even though he may be physically stronger than most girls, this doesn't mean that he is any more gifted than them. She may be faster than him or more agile than him. He should look at every girl as an individual. He can learn as much if not more from them than he can from a lot of boys.*

## GUIDE 9

I tell my son that he should look at every girl as an individual. He can learn as much if not more from them than he can from a lot of boys.

## Where are the Black Men?

Black women frequently ask: Where are the black men? They know that the gantlet of American abuses— prison, disease, early death—takes a fearful toll on black men. The prospects for some black men are so dreary they have been called an "endangered species."

A black woman is aware that by the time she reaches age thirty there will ten less black men for every 100 black women. At forty and beyond, the numbers dwindle even more.

Black women understand this. But, they do not understand the lack of commitment. Many are haunted by the specter of losing more black men to interracial relations. And while some seek love and comfort in a relationship with non-black men, most still prefer to build solid relationship with a black man.

Still, they are painfully aware that times have changed. Years ago, in the South, black men who had (or were accused of) sexual relations with white women were often charged with rape and lynched or executed in prison. It took no more than the word of a white female. But with the legal restraints removed, black men no longer fear dating or marrying non-black women. If they do, many black women wonder where does this leave them?

PERRY—*For several years, the lady I had a serious relationship with was white. We had a lot in common. We were able to talk about anything and we usually agreed. But there were problems. When we were out, I would catch people staring at us—whites and blacks. It was like we were always under a microscope. We tried to ignore it, but it was difficult.*

*Sometimes there were little slights at restaurants and theaters. I couldn't say for sure that it was because I was black and she was white but I had my suspicions. I was always on guard. We came very close to getting married. But we didn't and I can't exactly say why. I can say that after we broke up I didn't feel that I had to go out and find another white girlfriend. Our relationship wasn't based on any color thing. It was based on love and shared interest. I was able to have the same kind of relationship with the lady that followed her. She is black and we are now married.*

More black men are marrying or dating non-black women but it does not mean that black male-female relations are in a hopeless state of disrepair. Nine out of ten black men marry black women. While black men—and women too—reserve the right to date or marry whomever they please, most also consider the realities of racism and the sentiments of many in the black community who frown on interracial marriages.

It is not a perfect world. Children of mixed marriages are often the targets of taunts and insensitive barbs from adults and their peers. But if fathers arm them with confidence, strength, self-esteem and identity; they can easily deflect the attacks. Is it worth the effort? Some think so.

ROBERT—*I don't think that color should be the standard for any relationship between a man and a woman. You can't control feelings. If a man and a woman love each other they are going to marry or have a relationship. And that's important because your first responsibility is to your children. The woman that you are with has to be a considerate and concerned mother. She may be white, Latino, Asian or whatever. If she has those qualities then the children will grow and develop properly.*

*Also, I don't think the world is framed only in black and white. Children need to learn about other cultures. I had a*

*Filipino girlfriend. My son learned a lot about Filipino cooking, culture, language and customs from her. This broadens him and better prepares him to deal with the different kinds of people that he will have to deal with as an adult.*

Now, let's look at the other side. Many black men do whatever it takes to develop a strong and loving relationship with a black woman. They believe they have an obligation to strengthen and preserve the black family. They are aware of the proud tradition of generations of black fathers who have faced the road-blocks of racism and oppression side-by-side with their women. Who, they ask, can better understand their problems? Who is better equipped to face the difficulties with them? Who better to build the bond of unity with them than a black woman?

LAWRENCE—*If a black man and woman could deal with each other when things were bad, then they can deal with each other now that things are relatively better and they have choices. I don't think that it's a sign of success for the black man to be with a white woman. I think it's a sign of maturity that when he is successful he maintains a relationship with a black woman. If he can do this, it will carry over into other areas of life. By that I mean, it can instill a sense of unity and willingness to support each other in business or the job market.*

Each year the National Council of Negro Women holds a Black Family Reunion. The millions of black men who attend are the best answer to the questions: Do black men want the best for their children and will they work to build their relationship with their mate? As black fathers, they come together to gain strength from one another and to inspire one another. They come together to give advice and receive it.

Their goal is to keep their children safe in an unsafe world and their relations healthy in an unhealthy world. To succeed black fathers must wear many hats. They must be part counselor, educator, motivator, psychologist and personal relations specialist. Some attain their goals. Some do not. But the important thing is many try.

---

**GUIDE 10**

I say that if a black man and woman could deal with each other when things were bad, then they can deal with each other now that things are relatively better and they have choices.

---

# 4

# I Didn't Make the Baby by Myself

We didn't think very much about it at the time. It seemed to the three of us a natural thing to talk about our fathers. Jimmy was excited because his father had just bought him a new model airplane. He gleefully told us how the two of them had spent the afternoon putting it together. When he finished, I told him that my father played in the national guard band and that he let me sit on the bandstand while he and the other musicians practiced.

As we chatted away, we noticed that Harold was silent. He had a forlorn look. And then we remembered. Harold lived with his mother and two sisters. Neither of us had ever seen his father. And Harold never talked about him. We changed the subject.

HOWARD—*It still comes down to whether a man has a job that he is secure in. This is what makes a man feel like a man. It builds up his confidence and self-esteem. If he can't make it financially it does something to him. He feels that his wife or girlfriend thinks less of him. He gets negative vibrations in the home and outside of it.*

*Next thing you know there are problems. He might start drinking, pick fights with his wife, and find excuses to stay away from the home.*

*Then one day he leaves and doesn't come back. That's why it's so important for a man to know that his woman supports him. If she believes in him, he will believe in himself.*

African-Americans know the Harolds among them quite well. Their numbers grow larger. So large that one out of two black children lives with one parent. To say this is not to agree with those sociologists who ignore racism and poverty and falsely compare the family status of low income blacks to the white middle-class. They paint a lop-sided picture of black family decay. It is merely to say that the strains of America have caught up with many black fathers.

PERRY—*I didn't stop being a father when I separated from my wife. I tried to call at least once a week. I would send a card or a note to my daughter, encouraging her in school or with her music lessons. I treated my visitation times like they were gold. If I was going to pick her up at 3:00 p.m. to take her to a movie or something, I got there at 2:45 p.m. I was always early. It had a magic effect. She was all smiles.*

It's not just numbers. Any single black mother can tell you that life is no crystal stair. Usually, she is less skilled, less educated and poorer. Yet she is still a mother who wants the best for her children. It tears at her heart when she can't give it to them. It is not hard to see why. The two income family has become the standard by which American society gauges success.

Many know that the trouble-free, eternally happy Ozzie and Harriet home was little more than a concoction of a generation of silent bliss. The husbands drank, the children rebelled and the wives suffered silently in their forced confinement in the role of cheerful housewife. Since there was only one wage earner, the family probably always needed money.

Without the income from her Ozzie, the single black mother always needs money. The point is that two incomes are necessary to really make it in America. Yet only one in three black single mothers will receive any child support. The income of absentee fathers can mean the difference between financial survival and disaster. Their presence is important, but so are their dollars.

LAWRENCE—*A lot of guys claim that they don't have enough money to take care of their kids. That's a bunch of nonsense. They aren't being honest. I know women that raise four or five children with just a welfare check and food stamps. You can't tell me that a bachelor living by himself is making it with money less than her. The only excuse I can see for not paying the full amount of child support is if a man has another family. But even then he can go to court and get an adjustment so that he can meet his responsibilities on both ends.*

## GUIDE 11

I treat my visitation rights like gold. If I am scheduled to pick up my daughter at 3:00 p.m. to go to a movie or something, I get there at 2:45 p.m.

## Every Goodbye Ain't Goodbye

When the black father deserts the home, it makes good media copy and impressive sociological studies. Many can say, "Ah hah," that proves that the black man is an irresponsible cad. The truth is that black men who do abandon their wives and children are the minority. Most black couples end marriages the same way most whites, Latinos and Asians in America do. They separate or they divorce and the reasons are pretty much the same. They disagree on finances, children, sex, who picks up the dirty clothes, who wants to watch what TV program or whatever else they can conjure up.

For black families these problems are only the beginning. They face extra pressures from unemployment, discrimination, and the endless array of insults and slights that come daily with being black in America. Although it's a volatile mix that can destroy the ties between any black couple, the explosion doesn't have to be fatal.

HOWARD—*I always tell myself, 'I'm going to make this marriage work.' I try to think before I open my mouth when a problem comes along. But I'm a realist. There are times when you can't keep quiet or be diplomatic. You say things that are blunt, brutal, even cruel. But it's better to get it out rather than holding it in and letting it simmer.*

*If we still can't come to some sort of compromise, then I consider getting outside help. It doesn't have to be a professional counselor. It could be a close relative or friend that has the maturity and experience to see both sides. They can sometimes see things that a couple will miss and can say it without the other getting angry and feeling that they are being picked on. Several times, I've tried this and it has at least allowed my wife and I to talk calmly and rationally.*

There were nights when I heard my father and mother arguing. They always fought over little things that didn't make much sense to me. But they acted as if the fate of the world hung on the outcome of their personal battle. Neither was prepared to give an inch. It was a true test of wills. One day their battle reached a truly epic scale. My father was losing ground fast. He stormed from the house, shouting to my mother that this was the last time she would see him. BAM, the door slammed!

I was worried. The fierce tone in his voice bespoke of a certain finality. Did he really mean it? Was he never going to come back? What would we do? Night came and my father hadn't returned home. I did not sleep well. All I could think of was what if he meant it? The next morning, I heard my father's voice. He and my mother were talking quietly in the kitchen. When I heard them laugh, I was relieved. I knew that the storm had passed. They would have more blow-ups but the next morning, he was always there.

Most black men do not break and run at the first hint of problems. They do try to work out their problems. They talk. They listen. They negotiate. They compromise. They may seek outside help. This takes enormous strength and maturity. It also takes a willingness to change.

LAWRENCE—*A lot of men feel frustrated when problems come up. They feel that their woman is getting the better of them in a situation and they don't like it. They may not have the education or the verbal skills to deal with her. They think that since they are the man the woman should not get the upper hand. There are times when I feel that. When that happens I like to change-up. I may leave for a few hours and go to a movie, visit a friend, take a walk or a drive. I try to collect my thoughts, gather my strength and give the situation a chance to cool out.*

*Sometimes I will suggest that maybe we should put the problem on hold and do something completely different; something we would never dream of doing. I'll give an example. We wanted to buy a certain item and we couldn't agree on how much we should spend. So rather than keep arguing over it, I said why don't we go find a spa, get a massage or relax in the Jacuzzi. It was spontaneous. We did. We didn't talk about the issue the whole time. It worked. We were able to come back to it a day later and resolve it.*

Some black fathers do reach a point of no-return. Once they close the door, they will never open it again. But feelings are another matter. They can't turn them on and off like a water faucet. Most black fathers find it impossible to stop caring as a  single black mother told an interviewer:

*The children's fathers are always somewhere in the back-ground . . . coming, knocking, and going through all these changes. If I were a man and I married a woman, I wouldn't want her ex-husband or ex-man to come knocking on the door saying, 'Can I see my kids?' But that's the problem you have to face.*

In her own way, this single black mother confirms this.

ROBERT—*When a man and woman split, I don't think that men hold grudges as long. They are more ready to forgive; whether it was their fault or the woman's fault. I think the problem is that some women don't forgive as easily. They want to hurt or punish the man. She takes the attitude, 'Well you hurt me, you did this to me. I don't ever want to see you again.' So the man is not welcome to come and visit his kids.*

*If he sends money, the mother may not let the child know that it came from him. If he calls, she might not let them talk to him. If he sends them a letter, she might not give it to them. Those women should not let their feelings blind them to the fact that the children need support from their father. The children also need to maintain physical and emotional ties with him.*

There is the popular notion that black fathers leave the home and run the streets day and night. They spend money recklessly. They party every night. They chase women relentlessly. They rarely think about their families and children. Some are like that. But many others aren't.

Parenting from afar is tough and demanding. The wise black father understands that children still need nourishing and emotional support. They must keep the doors open and maintain constant contact through the critical years of their children's growth and development. If they are not there during these years, they have no right to boast about or claim credit for their son's or daughter's achievement in scholarship, music, dance, art or sport. It is too late.

ROBERT—*A father who feels he has to leave should either arrange for his children to live with him part of the time or take them with him on a full-time basis. I say this because he is usually better off financially than the woman. He can provide the strong male role model and discipline that boys especially need. The man can't use the excuse that he doesn't have time or that he can't find someone to take care of the kids. Most women work eight hours a day and they*

*seem  to manage this. I also think that he can cook, clean and*
*wash, too. If he doesn't know how, he should learn.*

---

## GUIDE 12

I feel that a father who leaves the home should
arrange for his children to live with him part of
the time or take them with him on a full-time
basis.

---

## Mommy and Daddy Too?

More black children than ever are living with their
fathers. While the number overall is still small in
comparison to those who live with their mothers, it's
still worth noting. The trend began in the 1960s. If it
continues into the twenty-first century, one out of
three children may live in a single parent household.
The difference will be that the parent will as likely be
the father as the mother. Why are more black fathers
willing to assume the responsibility of dual parent that
black women have borne for decades? Some men have
little choice. They have lost their spouses through
death, incarceration or desertion.

Others have made a conscious choice to be both
father and mother to their children following their

*ROBERT —It was funny the way people reacted to me when my kids lived with me. Relatives would always ask me: 'How are you doing?' 'Who's looking after the kids?' 'You sure you don't need a cook or a housekeeper?' My friends even stopped calling because they thought that I wouldn't have time to go and have a little fun. It was like everybody was shocked that a man could take care of his kids without a woman and still lead a normal life.*

*After awhile, they could see that I kept a clean house, the kids were fed properly, they always had the right clothes, and they were getting to school on time. Most of the places I went, my kids were with me. They realized that my kids weren't suffering being alone with me.*

Black men find the new world of parenting strange and bewildering. It is their first experience with child caring. They discover what women have always known; being a parent is a full time job. A job with no lunch breaks, leisure time or vacations. It is a job that does not pay wages or advance a career.

The pay-off cannot be measured by dollars. The pay-off is far greater than a promotion or a raise. The pay-off comes with a hug, an admiring look, a searching question from their daughter or son. The pay-off comes when they take their daughter or son to the park or the museum. The pay-off comes at night when their daughter or son asks them to tuck them in and read a bedtime story to them.

The pay-off comes as they watch their son or daughter receive their high school or college diploma. The pay-off comes when their daughter or son achieves in business, a profession or a trade. The pay-off comes when they realize their daughter or son has become a mature, responsible adult. The pay-off comes when their daughter or son puts their arm's around them and says, "Dad, I love you."

Is there a better pay-off?

PERRY—*At first, I was a little worried that having my kids with me, I might have to cut back on some of my outside activities. But I haven't missed a beat. When I want to go, we go.*

Sooner or later the black father who decides to raise his children will fall in love and probably remarry. Now there is a new presence in his children's lives. How will his children accept their "new mommy"? Fathers want to help their children make the necessary adjustments. They want the transition to be smooth. Often, it isn't.

Shortly, after my marital break-up, I began dating my present wife. There were warning signals almost from the beginning that things weren't right. When she visited, my son would immediately go outside or close the door of his room. At dinner, he would gulp his food down and rush from the room. He would not give me phone messages when she called.

He became less talkative and more withdrawn. Discussions between us were one-sided. I talked and his answers were monosyllabic. After his grades plummeted and his interest in school dropped below zero, I knew it was time to take action. It took many discussions and several counseling sessions before he could finally tell me, "I liked it better the way things were before."

It was finally out in the open. He was acting out the deep resentment that he harbored toward me for starting a new relationship. He felt threatened. By then, I had remarried and my wife understood the problem. She was patient and supportive. Her actions showed him that she was not trying to replace his mother. This helped us break through the barriers. He also saw that I loved him the same. It was a test for all.

PERRY—*A short time before I met my second wife, I took my daughter to a counselor. I wanted her to be able to express her feelings about us. I didn't want her to bury her feelings, because they always come out negatively later. I also wanted her to understand that because I was not with her mother it didn't mean that I was a bad daddy, or that mommy was a bad mommy.*

*This helped a lot later on when I met my present wife. The kids seemed more open and accepting of her. They knew that their mother was still their mother. So they didn't feel like they were betraying or being disloyal to her by being friendly with my present wife.*

The thought of a child without its father is painful. We know about the poverty and the hardship of family break-up. But we also think of the nurturing that children may miss when a father is absent. We empathize with the noble struggle of the single mother to hold her family together. Still, those who say the black family is dead are mourning prematurely. It has shown a resilience over time that defies the odds.

Many black children from single parent homes have gone on to successful careers in business, the professions and the trades. Some of them have been outstanding leaders, such as Malcolm X, who lost his father when he was six, but never lost his proud memory of him. Many of these women and men can thank their fathers who, though out of the home, were not out of their lives. These black fathers proved that love can conquer adversity.

# 5

# AN AFROCENTRIC PASSAGE TO ADULTHOOD

The small group of young boys sat nervously in a circle in the middle of the forest. They did not speak to each other. Each one was deeply immersed in his thoughts and perhaps fears of what was to come. The men of their village had brought them to this place. For the past week, the boys hunted and shared meals with the men. In the evenings, they listened as their elders told them stories of the village's past. Now as they sat in the circle in the forest, they prepared for the final ceremony. They would be circumcised. This was their last hurdle in their passage to manhood.

In West African society, nothing was more important than the rite of passage to adulthood. All young men were required to go through the training and then the ceremony. It was the crowning achievement for African youth. "As new men," says Alex Haley, "they must therefore learn to treat everyone with the same respect, and—as the foremost of their manhood duties—to protect the welfare of every man, woman, and child as they would their own." It was an awesome but necessary responsibility.

ROBERT—*My children know that I have certain standards. They must look me in the eye when they talk to me. They must speak clearly and intelligently. I do not tolerate lies. If they tell me the truth when they've done something wrong, then I may not punish them. It makes them think. It makes them understand that truth and honesty have its own rewards. I try to be open with people and not to prejudge them. I listen to what they say. I want my kids to do the same.*

*I keep the house clean. I dress neatly. I try to be punctual when I pick them up from school or the movies. I try to be* consistent and fair in enforcing the rules. I expect them to be the same way.

If one looks closely at the lives of the men and women who have made lasting contributions to the African-American experience, they see that they had the same qualities. They were independent. They had a strong sense of self. They were dedicated to their people. It could not be any other way. The struggle for justice and equality demanded vast inner reserves of moral and spiritual strength. These qualities did not mystically fall from the sky. They spring from the ancient and traditional humanistic values and customs of the African past. They were nurtured along the way by those who loved and cared for them.

ROBERT—*A lot of things I don't have to talk with my children about. They are a mirror reflection of their parents. If I don't curse, steal, lie, cheat and not deal with people with respect, they will pick up on that. If I am honest in my dealings with others, they can see that, too.*

*I was at the store with my son and a man in front of us in the check-out line dropped a fifty dollar bill on the floor. He didn't see it. I picked it up and gave it back to him. He thanked me and offered to give me ten dollars for returning it. I told him to forget it. It wasn't that I wouldn't have liked to have the ten or even the fifty dollars, but I knew that my son, even though he didn't say a word, was watching.*

## GUIDE 13

I think children are a mirror reflection of their parents. If I don't curse, steal, lie, cheat and disrespect people; they will pick up on that.

## Which Value System?

### *This?*

Respect
Responsibility
Positive reinforcement
Self-sufficiency
Love and protection of children and family
Cooperation
Accountability
Justice
Fair play
Trust
Value on learning skills
Long term goals
Encouragement of creativity
Spirituality

## Or This?

Individualism
Greed
Untruthfulness
Manipulation
Distrust
Hostility
Selfishness
Live for the moment

HOWARD—*My kids couldn't stay out until all hours of the night. I didn't care if they were sitting on the front steps. That was the rule and they had to follow it. Sometimes this would cause them problems. They would always complain that they were the first at a party and the first to leave. But they got the message and appreciated it. I know because once a friend bragged to my son that his parents let him stay out as long as he pleased. My son told him, 'Evidently they don't think too much of you.'*

"Daddy, what was your best Christmas?" My eleven-year-old daughter put me on the spot. I had to pause and think. Was it the Christmas I got the electric train? Or the Christmas when I got the baseball mitt? Maybe it was the Christmas as a grown-up when I played the big spender and gave my friends and relatives the jewelry, clothes or gadgets they wanted.

Then I remembered the Christmas when Kenny,

the poor kid whose family lived in the basement apartment down the street from us, got his first Christmas tree. It seemed a miracle at the time. Kenny and I were passing the neighborhood Christmas tree lot when we spotted two boys trying to steal a tree. We shouted for them to drop it, and they ran away.

The grateful lot owner looked hard at us. He ran his eyes slowly over Kenny's threadbare jacket and worn shoes. He said "You want it, it's yours." We grabbed the tree and ran to Kenny's house. His father met us at the door. He was a proud and stern man who did not tolerate foul language or disrespect from his children. I never heard Kenny utter a curse word.

His first question was, "Where did you get this from?" as he looked at the tree and us suspiciously. He listened as we excitedly told him the story. After a long moment of silence, he told us to wait there. He was going to talk to the owner of the lot.

He shot us a no-nonsense look on his way out the door that told us our story had better be true. We were nervous. Shortly afterwards, he returned. The huge grin on his face told everything. The tree stayed. That Christmas would be a special one for his family.

Did my daughter understand the message of the

story? Her smile was my answer. It was a smile for Kenny and his father. It was a smile for me.

ROBERT—*I tell my son, 'Your attitude and how you carry yourself means everything.' When you go for an interview, they are evaluating you as soon as you walk through the door. They are looking at how you dress, how you walk and stand. Your body language tells a person a lot about you before you even open your mouth. They are wondering: Is this a person I can work with? Does this person have integrity? Are they honest and reliable?*

I'm pretty sure my father wouldn't know what to say if I had asked him whether he had a plan to raise me. Parenting is not like plotting a battlefield campaign. Few parents ever sit down and draw up a formal blueprint for their children's development. But if children are to have a safe passage to adulthood, there must be a plan—a set of rules which they insist that their children live by.

HOWARD—*I don't care how good you are as a parent. When they get into their teens you will lose them for a time. But, if you built a strong enough foundation, you'll reel them back in later.*

Their plan rests on the values that they were taught and that worked for them. But children are smart. They watch their parents closely. They take their cues from what they do—not what they say. Parents have little choice. If they want to smooth out the bumps in their children's passage to adulthood, they must follow their plan themselves.

HOWARD—*The kids pretty much knew my work schedule. I left home about the same time, and tried to get back close to the same hour in the evening. I gave them my card with my phone number in case of an emergency. Oftentimes I would call home after school, to see if they were there. I'd ask them about school and their lessons. I made it clear that if they had a problem with their homework they should ask me questions. If I couldn't answer it, we would check the encyclopedia or send a note to the teacher telling him or her the specific problem or question and asking for help. I thought it was important to maintain a presence and connect with them in some way every day.*

## GUIDE 14

I left for work at about the same time each day, and tried to get home close to the same time. I gave my kids my card with my phone number in case of emergency. It was important that they knew where I was.

# Say It Loud, I'm Black and I'm Proud

"Say it loud, I'm black and I'm proud." Those who lived through those years, can't forget them. It was a time when blacks called each other brother and sister—and meant it. The 1960s were an era of discovery and revelation. African-Americans took pride in their past. They were confident about the present. They had a sense of destiny for the future. They believed they could make America a better place to live for themselves and their children. The spirit of the past should be the spirit of the present.

PERRY—*I make sure that my daughter has a complete set of black Barbie dolls. I buy her and my son books on black history. I read to them passages from it and we discuss it. I also have a series on the great empires of Africa. We discuss that, too. I take them to as many black and African art exhibits and performances that I can. I always ask them if they understand what they are looking at. If they say they do, I ask them a few questions to make sure they really do understand. I don't want them to leave without having a basic understanding of the significance of the event.*

The Redbill Oxpecker stands on top of the Rhinoceros. It is a small bird, but it is secure and confident. It should be. It is standing on the shoulders of a giant.

I can say the same. During the first few years, my father worked at the post office, black men were not allowed to hold positions as window clerks. That wasn't good enough for my father. When they gave the clerk's test my father took it. He didn't pass. He took it again and again. It took some time, but eventually he became the first black clerk in his district. He didn't have to persist. He had a secure job that paid fairly well. Why did he keep taking the test? His answer: "But what about those who would come after me"?

EARL HUTCHINSON, SR.—*In those days the National Guard band unit I belonged to was segregated. This made us more determined to show what we could do. We rehearsed and rehearsed. Every man was proficient not only with his instrument but with his marching steps. On parade day, the men would wear their best dress uniforms. Their shirts were pressed, shoes shined, ties straight, and their hats centered. Not a stitch was out of place. Their horns were polished and shined so bright that when the sun hit them you'd blink.*

*They marched in perfect step, with their heads erect and eyes straight ahead. They didn't play a wrong note. They put on a first rate show. They knew that all eyes were on them. They wanted everybody to know that they were not only just as good, but better than anybody else. Even if they didn't get the recognition from the whites, they knew it in their hearts.*

We stand on the broad and powerful shoulders of the black fathers who took pride in their people. They prepared us. They sacrificed for us. They fought for us. They broke down the barriers of segregation and injustice for us. They opened the doors of opportunity that many of us walk through. We stand on the shoulders of giants.

PERRY—*My brother and my mother are always talking to the kids about their family. They tell them stories and they show them pictures of family members and tell stories about them. We bought the 'Roots' series and showed that to them. After that, the kids put together a family album with captions that give a little history of each of the relatives. When they finished, they sent away for a genealogical kit to try to trace their family history even further back than slavery.*

Marcus Garvey said it best. A people without a past is like a tree without roots. Every black leader before and after Garvey has paid homage to Africa. They understand that the black experience did not begin with slavery. For there were African kingdoms, empires, political, social and economic systems centuries before the existence of America. Over the millennia of time, the intellectual, artistic and scientific discoveries of Africans enriched the world. The search to rediscover that past is eternal.

ROBERT—My *three sons have African names. The oldest is named: OSOFU SAID. It's Ashanti and it means minister of peace. My middle son is named: KAMSI. It's a derivative of Kumasi. That's the name of a large city in West Africa. It means "to come together." My youngest son is named KALIF. It means one who has blessings bestowed upon him. As soon as they were old enough, I explained the meaning and the importance of their names.*

---

## GUIDE 15

I think it's important that my brother and my mother are always talking to the kids about their family. They show them pictures and tell them stories. The kids then put together their own family album.

---

## Keeping the Faith When Others Don't

When Israel was in Egypt's land,
Let my people go
Oppressed so hard they could not stand,
Let my people go

Go down, Moses,

Way down in Egypt's land,
Tell old Pharaoh
To let my people go

Africans believed deeply in their GODS. They were
kind and they watched over them. They gave them
strength and courage. They steered them on the right
course through life. Some called their Gods, *Bosumtwe.*
Some called them *watra mama.* Some called them *Dam-
balla.*

They talked to them in the trees, the wind, the earth
and the water. They brought the warmth of the sea-
sons. They brought the rain. They nourished the soil.
They were there during the planting and the harvest-
ing. They were present in the spirit of their ancestors.
Always they gave thanks to them.

African-Americans never lost that belief. Their spiritualism lay deep in African traditions. The violence
and oppression of slavery could not destroy that belief.
Religion has always been more than just a refuge from
the storms of life. Religion has been the rock on which
African-Americans have built their struggle for freedom and dignity.

In *The Souls of Black Folks*, W.E.B. DuBois spoke of
this as "Of the faith of our fathers." He understood the

profound collective renewal power of religion: "Back of this still broods silently the deep religious feeling of the real Negro heart, the stirring, unguided might of powerful human souls who have lost the guiding star of the past and seek in the great night a new religious ideal."

PERRY—*I'm a Catholic, but during the year, I might take my kids to several different churches. I want them to see the different types of services that churches have. I think that this gives them a better picture of how people worship. They can understand that even though people may call God by different names, they still have basically the same beliefs.*

> My God is a rock in a weary land
> My God is a rock in a weary land
> Shelter in a time of storm

I knew his words by heart, "If you're well enough to talk, you're well enough to go to church." It seemed I could never get sick enough to convince my father to let me skip church. As a deacon in the Woodlawn African Methodist Episcopal Church in Chicago, my father took his duties very seriously. He was one of the first to arrive, and the last to leave. He helped with the collections. He greeted people and escorted them to their seats. He assisted the pastor.

The services were long and the hours seemed to drag by. I felt like screaming "get me out of here!" Instead, I sat straight up in my seat and dutifully sang every hymn as my father held the book and ran his finger over the lines.

After the service ended, he stayed around to talk with some of the other deacons. Most of the children had left by then, so there was no one for me to play with. Only after he had a final word with the pastor was I sure we could go home—until next Sunday.

LAWRENCE—*There's more to church than just going and listening to a sermon. Your children learn how to interact with people, participate in activities and to be a part of an organization. It's good early training that will stay with them through life. This is why I encouraged my daughter to take part in as many activities at church as possible. She joined the choir, bible study class and the girl's track team. Even though she didn't stay very long with each group, it gave her experience in cooperating and working with other people.*

Nat Turner, Henry Highland Garnet, Alexander Crummell, Samuel Ward, Bishop Henry Turner, Bishop Archibald Carey, Dr. Benjamin Mays, Dr. Martin Luther King, Jr., The Honorable Elijah Muhammad and Minister Malcolm X. It is no coincidence that religious leaders have been the towering figures in the black freedom movement. These men believed deeply in the words of the old black spiritual: "let my people go." They knew that religion was a unifying and galvanizing force for change. They believed that religion at its best could instill the values of truth, righteousness and, yes, love.

ROBERT--*When I sent my son to a religious school, I knew that I was going to have to make a greater commitment of my time to the church and school programs. But that was OK. I didn't have any problems attending the special activities and events they had. I even became one of the coaches on the basketball team. My son also joined the team. I figured that this was a good chance for us to participate together in church and school programs. It seemed to bring us closer together.*

## GUIDE 16

I encouraged my daughter to take part in as many activities at church as possible. She joined the choir, bible study class and the track team. It gave her experience in co-operating and working with people.

# This Hurts Me More Than It Hurts You

"This hurts me more than it hurts you." We've all heard our parents say this, as the switch or belt sinks deep into our skin and we yelp with pain and wonder why we're crying and they aren't? To us, they were the meanest persons in the world. But the truth, is when they punished us, they hurt, too. Discipline is an art that, if handled properly, can produce results.

Only, who's to say what is proper? Proper is certainly not abuse or brutality. Black parents have often been accused of not sparing the rod when it comes to disciplining their children. They are not graduates of the school of indulgent parenting.

Some Black parents fear that if their children are rebellious or defiant they will get into trouble with the authorities. So they use punishment to teach submission. Some react to the pressures and stresses of daily living and take it out on their children. Some believe that punishment is the way to teach respect and correct behavior. Others just simply don't know anything else to do.

ROBERT—*I used to beat my sons when they were small. I would grab them and shake them as hard as I could. It worked. They were afraid of me. Now I don't even have to raise my voice. If I say go do your work, I don't have to repeat it again. They do it.*

That's one way. Here's another.

LAWRENCE—*It would be easy for me to take a belt and flail away at them. But I don't think that does much good. I don't want them to fear me or resent me. I want them to understand why what they did was wrong. I choose to talk to them. I sit down with them and ask them questions about their actions. I try to get them to see that what they did was wrong. I give them examples of how people do things that hurt other people. I want them to learn for themselves how to judge right from wrong. I want them to make decisions for themselves and be responsible for their actions. I won't always be there with a switch in my hand.*

While, there are no exact rules for discipline, it's worth remembering the "Be's":

Be calm
Be clear
Be consistent
Be exact
Be objective
Be purposeful
Be a discussant

Better yet, black fathers can head off problems before they become problems. When children (adults too) do things right. Praise them. It's called positive reinforcement. Again, remember the "Be's":

Be encouraging
Be praiseful
Be respectful
Be supportive

PERRY—*If my kids do something wrong I follow a three step plan.*

• *I tell them 'Don't do that.'*

• *I tell them 'Don't do that.' I show or explain to them why it's wrong.*

• *I tell them 'Don't do that.' I show or explain to them why it's wrong. I remind them that I warned them twice before and then I punish them. My youngest son may get a spanking. Since my daughter is older, I will forbid her to do something she likes, such as listening to music, watching TV or visiting friends.*

What if children don't agree with the rules they are being disciplined for breaking? If they think they are being treated unjustly or unfairly, discipline, no matter how well meaning, may backfire. The rules of respect and civility still apply, but the door for discussion and dialogue must be kept open. Just as black fathers can teach their children, they can learn from them, too.

It's always good to recall the example of Dr. King. He broke the rules that were unfair to African-Americans. He knew the consequences and he was willing to accept them. He was neither bitter nor hostile. He wanted justice only. He was disciplined.

LAWRENCE—*I challenge my kids a lot. I want them to think for themselves and to accept responsibility for their actions. I tell them that there are rules and if you break them you must be willing to pay the price. Everybody has to be accountable to someone for what they do. You can't blame your father, mother, brothers or sisters. It's on you when things go wrong.*

*To give an example, we had a rule that my kids could not receive calls after 8:00 p.m. I felt this was time that should be quiet time for them to read. Shortly after my son turned thirteen, he started staying on the phone after 8:00. The first couple of times I ignored it. The next time, I sat down with him and reminded him of the rule. He protested.*

*My first thought was to put him on punishment. But I*

*complete his studies and that he could read the same number of books in less time. I said OK. He could take calls later. I didn't warn him about his grades or school. That was understood. There wasn't a problem.*

---

**GUIDE 17**

I don't think taking a belt and flailing away at my kids does much good. I don't want them to resent me. I want them to understand why what they did was wrong.

---

## Role Models

It's another one of those most asked questions: "Who do you admire most"? Usually people choose a prominent personality or a celebrity. They don't really know how these people lead their lives. They're popular, so they pick them.

The search for the ideal role model should not be a popularity contest. Role models come in all sizes and shapes. They are all around us. There is really no such thing as the "ideal." Nearly everyone at times displays the qualities we admire: Compassion, strength, generosity, determination, honesty, and accomplishment. If black fathers showcase those qualities in their own lives, their children may too.

LAWRENCE—*My grandfather could not read, but he was a very knowledgeable and practical man. I liked to talk with him. He always seemed to have the right answers to my questions. When I had a problem, he would take time and help me work it through. He was never too busy to listen to me. I think he knew so much because he was speaking from life's experiences. I've always felt that it's important to listen to people like that. You can learn so much from them.*

They've made movies about him. They talk about him in poems and song lyrics. They show him on the news. He's a pimp. He's a pusher. He's a player. He's a con artist. He's a gangster. He has become the universal symbol of black men. Beware. He is not a role model. He is a distorted creation of American negativism.

PERRY—*I don't put posters or pictures of anyone on my walls. That's because I don't think it's good to idolize anyone. I think you should look for the qualities that are good in everyone and then make examples of them for your children. If a friend gives my daughter a present, I use that as an example of warmth and generosity. If she reads about* an athlete or entertainer who has made a donation to charity or helped out with some cause I always point that out to her.

Finding a role model is not a simple task. Our heroes sometimes do harmful things that betray our trust. There are others whom we want to admire but aren't quite sure about. This was James Baldwin's dilemma as he tried hard to sort out his feelings toward his father. A dilemma that even death could not resolve:

*The minister who preached my father's funeral sermon was one of the few my father had still been seeing as he neared his end. He presented to us in his sermon a man whom none of us had ever seen—a man thoughtful, patient and forbearing. A Christian inspiration to all who knew him. A model for his children.*

*This was not the man they had known, but they scarcely expected to be confronted with HIM. This was in a sense, deeper than questions of fact. The man they had not known may have been the real one.*

Children may never ask, but they often wonder who is that man they call their father.

ROBERT—*I believe I am the best role model for my sons. I take care of them. I take them to school. I help them with their homework. I take them to basketball practice, tutoring and church. We eat together, play together and pray together. I am the most influential person in their lives and they look toward me. That's the way it should be.*

Bringing a child to adulthood is a major undertaking for black fathers. Much of the time they travel through uncharted waters with no buoy markers to guide them. They have to be the arbiters of what is right and wrong for their children. The Africans took the passage so seriously that they called it "manhood training." The old folks simply called it teaching manners. They were speaking of the same things: cooperation, honesty, self-awareness and commitment to achievement. On their journey to adulthood, these are the qualities that we want our youth to show.

# 6

# DISCOVERING 'HIM': A TALK WITH MY FATHER

Like James Baldwin, most of us want to know who is this man we call "father"? Is he the man that he seems or is there something else about HIM that we don't know? We know that he had a life before we were born. But what kind of life?

Most of us will never ask. Partly because we put our fathers on such a distant pedestal that they become larger than life. But then we may not ask because we suspect that there are hidden compartments in their lives where painful secrets are buried deep and truths are blurred in the mists of time.

Our fathers may have done things that they want to forget. We should not be surprised. As Oscar Wilde said, young men must commit terrible sins so that as old men they can have terrible regrets.

Still, if we are lucky and our fathers are still with us, we owe it to ourselves to take them down from the pedestal and talk to them about their lives. I don't mean just listening to them tell of playful reminiscences. I mean their experiences and encounters. This may require a gentle nudge or even a hard push. But it's important because they are not only our fathers. They are our elders. And their past can serve as our signpost to the future.

Whether my father committed terrible sins and now has terrible regrets, I don't know. But I consider myself among those fortunate enough to have him here to ask him. He is now nearing his ninth decade of life. He has seen the triumphs and tragedies of this era. He has witnessed the wars, revolutions, social upheavals and major technological discoveries of the Twenti-eth Century.

He has lived through the days when African-Ameri-cans, in the immortal words uttered by Supreme Court Chief Justice Roger Taney in the Dred Scott decision in 1859, had no rights which a white man was bound to respect. He has seen the great movements of change that have guaranteed African-Americans their rights—at least on paper. He can remember when blacks were called: ex-slaves, colored, negro, Negro, black, Afro-American and African-American; everything, that is, except American.

So we talked. I asked him a few of the same ques-tions I asked the other black fathers I interviewed for *Black Fatherhood.* I believe that scattered among his recollections of yesterday's problems may be, just may be, a few of today's solutions.

But first let me take you on a detour through the personal life of the man that I call "father."

He was born at the turn of the century in the small town of Clarksville, Tennessee, located on the Cum-berland and Red Rivers in the Northwest corner of the state. Clarksville not only produced livestock and farm goods, it was a leader in the manufacture of snuff.

The town did not have a particularly violent history. In fact, most people there could remember only one lynching. But it was the South and the threat was always there. That was enough for my grandfather.

Jim Hutchinson (everybody called him Jim, never James) was fired by the dream that drove many blacks of his day. He would go North to escape the poverty and violence of the South, find a decent job, and live like a human being. The first chance he got, he took his wife and children and headed North. They settled in St. Louis. It didn't take him long to find out that the dream of freedom in the North was one more dream deferred for blacks.

St. Louis was just as segregated as Clarksville. The schools were just as ill-equipped, neighborhood housing was just as dilapidated, the police were just as brutal, public accommodations were just as closed, health was just as neglected, and blacks were just as poor.

Jim did whatever he could to earn a dollar. He labored in the livestock yards. He planted trees. He sold fruits and vegetables in the streets. It was touch-and-go most of the time for his family, but he persevered.

My father was too young to let racism or poverty disturb the innocence of his youth. After graduating from Sumner High School, which was the only school blacks could attend, he worked at odd jobs—delivery boy, elevator operator, junk yard laborer. Later, he got a job at the Post Office. Even though federal employment was completely segregated then, blacks considered this "a status job."

He might have stayed there, raised a family and settled down to a quiet life in St. Louis. But he had a vague itch, a yearning for more. He had outgrown the narrow provincialism of the St. Louis of those pre-Depression years. He knew there was a bigger world out there and he wanted to see it. For a young black this could only mean one of two places—Harlem or South Side Chicago.

He chose Chicago. He requested a transfer and he waited. When it came through, he said good-bye to his mother, father, three sisters and two brothers. After dutifully promising to keep in touch, visit and even send money occasionally; he boarded the train for Chicago and never looked back.

In the 1920s, Chicago was a rollicking wide open city, under the corrupt administration of Mayor Anton Cermack. Booze, prostitution, gambling and any other conceivable vice ruled the crime ridden, mob-run city. If you had the cash and connections everything was for sale. But since most blacks had neither, they found themselves nearly as poor and abused as they were on the plantations and farms that most of them had left in Mississippi, Arkansas or Tennessee.

Then the Great Depression hit. Many blacks did not know where their next check or meal would come from. Life for them became a bittersweet dance with survival. My father was lucky. He had a job that paid him in real money, meagre, yes, but real money, not script, as many workers then received.

There were other consolations. Like most blacks on Chicago's South Side, he lived in the area from 29th to 47th Street. The neighborhood was so tight-knit it was said that if you wanted to see a friend or relative from out of town you could stand on the corner of 35th and State Street and sooner or later they'd come by.

But the real delight was 47th Street. My father enjoyed the street's bustling night life, which then was second only to Harlem as the Mecca for black attractions. He could pop in at any one of the dozens of clubs, bars and speakeasies that lined the street.

There was the Grand Theater, the Vendome Theater, the Sunset Cabaret, the Apex Club and the Royal Garden. He could hear the sounds of Count Basie, Earl Hines, Fletcher Henderson, Fess Williams, Walter Barnes, Louis Armstrong, Cab Calloway, Duke Ellington, Muddy Waters or whatever big name black entertainer who happened to be passing through. Since all the clubs downtown and uptown were closed to blacks, they would play on 47th Street.

I remember seeing a well preserved picture of him. He was dressed dapperly in a double breasted suit. He had smooth skin, sparkling eyes and neatly trimmed moustache and what appeared to be a slightly licentious smile across his face. I'm sure he did his thing, and in the words of the ancient blues lament, "had his fun if he didn't get well no mo."

But it was only a matter of time. It happens to every would-be dandy. They meet someone who is just a little hipper, a little wiser, and a little stronger. She pierces the veil of male invincibility and brings him down to earth. It's called love.

When that happens marriage is usually close behind. My father met and married Lucille. Maybe they were too young, maybe they were too dumb, or just maybe it wasn't meant to be. Whatever the reason, it didn't last long.

The end came when my father received a panicky
call from his brother who lived close by. He told him to
get home right away because Lucille was moving all
the furniture out of the house. Only he really knows
how he felt. To hear him tell the story, he told his
brother, "let her have the junk, I'm going to get some
new furniture anyway."

He had better luck the second time. Thirty-seven
years later he was still married to my mother. As Hitler
poised to invade Poland, to start World War II, his first
child, my sister Earline, was born. A month after the
Japanese surrendered on the deck of the U.S.S. Missouri to end the war, I was born. I was in the first wave
of those who, a quarter century later, society would
fawningly call "the baby boomers." Of course, that
was years in the future. To my father, I was just another
mouth to feed. And if that wasn't enough, my half-
brother, Bobby, also lived with us during those years.

As America blissfully slumbered through the bobby
soxers, high school hops, Edsels and the anti-Commu-
nist McCarthy witch hunts of the 1950s, my father kept
his job at the Post Office. On the side, he dabbled in
ward politics to gain a few minor perks. With a growing family, he wanted a bigger and better place to live.
A home he could call his own. It took some doing, but

he finally found the ideal place. It was a three-story apartment building further South.

For any other family it would have been a simple thing, call the moving van, pack up the furniture, load the kids in the car and be on your way. But there was only one hitch. We were not any other American family. The apartment building was located in an all-white neighborhood and we were the first black family to buy there.

In those years, this building, like most others, had a restrictive covenant written into the deed. This meant simply that in perpetuity homeowners could not sell to blacks (one year later in 1948 the Supreme Court would declare restrictive covenants unconstitutional).

My father got around it by finding a "nominee." This was a sympathetic white person who would buy the home in their name and quit claim it over to the black buyer. It was risky business. The nominee might keep the money, the property owner might back out before the deal was closed, or angry homeowners could get an injunction to stop a black family from moving in. If that didn't work, they could resort to violence. In those days, more than one black family fled neighborhoods after their homes were burned and ransacked by white mobs.

Trouble began immediately. There were threats, shouts and even stones thrown at our door. This went on for a year. During that time, two policemen maintained a round-the-clock vigil in our lobby, and my father for the first and only time in his life kept a gun close by. Things finally settled down as more blacks moved into the neighborhood. By the time we moved seven years later, the neighborhood was practically all-black.

My father is a passionate music lover. He was a saxophonist for his National Guard band unit. His great joy was the evenings he spent at the Armory practicing with the band. When he took me with him, it was my joy, too. While the men belted out their hot practice numbers on the bandstand, I would roam the cavernous halls of the Armory in an army helmet, military belt and my play rifle, fighting imaginary battles with unseen enemies.

As the years passed, my parents grew restless. They heard stories about a new land of opportunity out West in California. They took a drive out there and fell in love with it. To my parents, the land of sunshine and oranges seemed like paradise. They had found yet another promised land.

When my father retired in the early 1960s, they

moved to California. They watched as their children grew to maturity. My brother joined the army. My sister began a career as an artist and a designer, and me, well I would spend a few years trying to figure out what I wanted to do.

But he was a patient man. He had made his peace with the world and was settling in to enjoy the golden years that America says its aging citizens are entitled to after a lifetime of sacrifice and struggle. Then tragedy struck. My mother died of cancer. It was a bitter loss. After nearly a lifetime together, he could not forget her.

There were days when I would drive out to the cemetery with him. He would carefully put flowers on her grave. While I walked back to the car he would linger for a few moments over her grave, I saw his lips faintly moving. They were talking. It was so very private. Only they would ever know what was said. She was very much alive and would always be.

Still, he was no different than any other man. He had physical and emotional needs that memories alone could not satisfy. He hungered for the warmth and caress that only a companion can bring. He got lucky again. He found a lovely lady who gives him the proper doses of affection, attention and when he needs it, his come-uppance. From what I can see, their married years have been good ones.

Now that you know something about this man that I call father, what does he think about some of the problems that face black men today?

# Interview

EARL, JR.—Tell me what works against black men as fathers?

EARL, SR.—*That's easy, no jobs. If a guy doesn't have any income, he can't support his family. Whose fault is that? Doesn't the government have some responsibility to find jobs for its people.? It's ridiculous. The government doesn't have any problem finding money to fight wars or take care of people in foreign countries, but it can't even take care of its own.*

*Back during the Depression, I remember stepping over guys sleeping on cardboard in Washington Park (on Chicago's South Side). They were everywhere. And they weren't just black, there were plenty of whites, too. They were all in the same boat. They couldn't take care of themselves, so how could they take care of families?*

*The Democrats saw that the only way they could help*

*these men and their families was to give them something; make jobs for them. They did. Pretty soon, you saw that more families were staying together when the man had a little something, and that was good.*

EARL, JR.—Those were different times, they didn't have the problem with drugs, high crime and delinquency that we do today.

EARL, SR.—*Maybe there wasn't a problem with drugs like now, but they did some of the same kind of stuff then. People got drunk, men beat their wives. And remember, if you were black back then, there were no laws to protect you. I mean you were just at the mercy of society. Things were bad and everybody knew it. But I think what made the difference was that we had more of a sense of pulling together. People were more religious then, we prayed a lot. We believed in God.*

*Also, we all lived together then. A guy might be a doctor or a lawyer. It didn't make any difference. He lived right next door to a janitor or porter. In the Post Office, we had guys who were college graduates, some even had Master's Degrees. It didn't make any difference. They would be working side by side with a guy who never finished high school. The kids had somebody they could look up to.*

EARL, JR.—It seems like people's values were different then.

EARL, SR.—*That's right. People cared more about each other. They took more of an interest in what their friends and neighbors were doing. Your neighbors were almost like part of your family. One time you got into a rock fight with some other kids and the police came and took you all down to the station. A neighbor who saw it called me right away and told me what happened. Right away, I went to the station, I was mad because there was really no reason for them to take you down, you were just kids.*

*When I got there several other parents were there too, so evidently somebody had called them. And it was kind of funny to hear everybody shouting at the police. I mean they were raising hell with them. The officers laughed and said they just wanted to scare you and the others a little. It wasn't funny to us, we got all of you out of there fast.*

EARL, JR.—How did that sense of caring carry over into your relationship with your wife?

EARL, SR.—*I'm not going to try and say that we didn't have our bad moments, every couple does. People aren't going to always be kissing and hugging each other. There's just too many things that can happen to change a person's attitude and mood. They might have a bad day at work. They might not be feeling well or they could be tired. They may have a problem with money. Anything. And they just don't feel like being lovey dovey. So there's going to be problems. That's just natural.*

*Its easy for people to be happy when things are going good, but what happens when the rough times come? That's the real test. If you truly love the other person, then you will respect them. That's important. If you respect them then you will take them seriously when they talk to you. You might not agree with what they have to say, and you might still want to do things your way, but you will listen. What they have to say may sit with you for a while—sometimes things take time to sink in—but eventually you will see that they might have something. Then you can reach some kind of compromise.*

EARL, JR.—Did that work with you?

EARL, SR.—*Most of the time. But sometimes, you get it in your head that you just want to get your way. That's natural too. And sometimes you should. But, like I say, if you love and respect the other person then you will come together. One may decide that this is one time when it is better to let the other person have their way even though you don't want to. That's hard, but a mature person can do it. They realize by giving a little here they may gain a lot later. A good general knows when to go forward and when to give ground. He knows that he'll eventually get it back.*

EARL, JR.—That really takes a lot of maturity to understand that?

EARL, SR.—*True, and there's one more thing on that. People would do a lot better if they didn't always expect so much of each other. This is what gets two people in trouble. They see things through their eyes and they try to make the other person see it the same way. They forget that the other person doesn't have the same eyes. I think in my day, we didn't always make those demands on each other and we didn't give the other person a lot of ultimatums.*

EARL, JR.—You did make demands on your children. You wanted them to be the best. Wasn't that why black parents valued education almost as much as they valued the church?

EARL, SR.—*We did. We knew that it was the only thing that really meant anything. There was never any such thing as sending report cards home. We went to pick them up. If there was a problem, we went up to the school the same day. If there was a conference with the teacher, the father went, too. More often than not, there were just as many fathers as there were mothers at school when they had some event.*

*In Chicago, a lot of black parents pulled their kids out of the public schools and put them in Catholic schools. I did that with you. The public schools were just so bad and the Catholics had a good reputation then. Many of these parents weren't making much money, and they had to sacrifice a lot to pay that tuition, but we were willing to do it because we knew that in the Catholic schools they were tough, and you would learn something.*

EARL, JR.—Speaking of learning something, one of the major problems that still affects African-Americans is lack of health care and information. Now with diseases such as AIDS, it's more important than ever to be informed. I don't know if this was an issue when you were raising your family . . . .

EARL, SR.—*It was an issue. I'm not talking about AIDS, because that wasn't known then. But there was Tuberculosis and Pneumonia and those diseases killed a lot of people. With sex you might get syphilis and gonorrhea, people died from that, too. What made it even worse, remember, was that we didn't have access to doctors and hospitals. People didn't have insurance and even if they could afford it, a lot of companies wouldn't write policies for blacks anyway.*

EARL, JR.—So what did people do?

EARL, SR.—*They used common-sense.*

EARL, JR.—What do you mean?

EARL, SR.—*If it was cold they didn't run around wearing a tee shirt and shorts like you see people doing now.*

*As soon as they felt a little weak, flu or something, they would sit or lie down. They tried not to let themselves get all worked up over every little thing. They knew how to take things in stride and relax.*

*They also had a lot of what we called the "remedies." Since most us came from the South, we knew how to cure ailments at home. We knew how to make cold and hot compacts; how to use herbs, tonics and vegetable roots. We also made lots of soups. When you or your sister got a cold and couldn't breathe, we'd boil a pan of hot water, squeeze some lemon in it, put a towel over your head to keep the steam in, and have you bend over it and breathe deeply the steam.*

EARL, JR.—Did it work?

EARL, SR.—*You never complained.*

EARL, JR.—I know drugs weren't a problem, but didn't everybody smoke and drink then?

EARL, SR.—*A lot of people did. I didn't.*

EARL, JR.—Why?

EARL, SR.—*When I was with the band, the guys would always get together afterward and drink. That's just what you were supposed to do. I tried to go along with them a few times, but the whiskey would make me so sick that I just couldn't get past that bad feeling. It was the same with smoking. It just didn't give me a good feeling, even though all my buddies smoked.*

*When I look around and see what it can do to you, I guess I was lucky that I didn't like to drink or smoke. It was good also because we never kept much liquor or any cigarettes around the house. You never saw us smoking or drinking. Maybe that's why you didn't pick up the habit.*

*It seems to me that if kids see their parents smoking and drinking then, unless they're exceptional, they're just naturally going to pick up those habits, too. So I think you were lucky that the stuff did make me sick .*

EARL, JR.—We've got another problem. Too many black kids are having kids, years ago that wasn't true . . .

EARL, SR.—*It was a little different. If a girl got pregnant and she wasn't married it was a big scandal. She almost couldn't be seen in public. Some parents would even send her away to live with an aunt, grandmother or relative in another town. But girls still got pregnant. It just wasn't openly talked about.*

*There weren't any classes or teachers that taught things*

like sex education. People were too afraid to even say the word. So it was something that was supposed to be taken care of in the home.

I don't know if this was good or bad, but many parents tried to put the fear of God in the girls. They'd tell them it was a sin to get pregnant, and God would punish them if they did. They tried to make them feel guilty. Maybe this wasn't the best way, but it seemed to work.

EARL, JR.—It seems like that put the whole burden on girls. It takes two to make a baby. Isn't it just as important, maybe even more important, to get the boys to accept responsibility for their actions.

EARL, SR.—*I'm just telling you that's the way people handled things then.*

EARL, JR.—But today . . .?

EARL, SR.—*Wait. Even then, if a man made a baby and he wasn't married, it was pretty well understood that the man had to marry the girl. It didn't make much difference how old he was. They had to get married. They called it a "shotgun wedding." The girl's father would find out who the boy was and come looking for him. There were a whole lot of weddings where the boy was dragged to the alter kicking and screaming.*

*For some guys it was too much, they might leave home, rather than go through all that. But a lot of times that didn't work. I knew some men who would track the guy to another city and one day show up on his doorstep. I knew a couple of guys who tried to run away and next thing I knew, they were back in Chicago married to the girl.*

EARL, JR.—I can't believe that a marriage like that could have any hope of lasting.

EARL, SR.—*You'd be surprised, many did. More often than not, the couple would stay together for years. It's funny how things work. Something you may be forced into and not like, over time you find out that it's right for you. All I know is that some guys I knew that got married like that stayed married and did right by their families.*

EARL, JR.—What if they didn't make it and the man left. You were talking before about jobs being the most important thing for a man to have. He might have to leave because he couldn't support his family.

EARL, SR.—*That's what happened to James (his brother). He didn't stay married hardly anytime to the woman he got pregnant. I don't know, maybe they weren't right for each other. I know James had the big problem with drinking so that it probably had something to do with it too.*

*He was a musician, too, so that didn't help since he was always on the road. But he cared enough about Jimmy (his son) to send money fairly regularly. And that was something then, because remember, there were no laws in those days that forced a man to pay.*

*He did something else. Do you remember who Jimmy stayed with while he was growing up?*

EARL, JR.—His Grandmother.

EARL, SR.—*That's right. I don't know how James worked it out. He knew that his mother—your grandmother—wanted to take him and so they worked it out. That was probably his way of making sure he was taken care of properly. Jimmy always called her mother. So he had that tie with his father. He never felt abandoned.*

EARL, JR.—So an absentee father can still be a father?

EARL, SR.—*Of course. Just because a man has left the home for good doesn't mean he isn't a father. In fact, when that happens, I would say that he probably should be more of a father then if he were there.*

EARL, JR.—What do you mean?

EARL, SR.—*Children tend to make a father that they*

*don't see regularly bigger than life. A lot of it's fantasy and more often they will be hurt and disappointed if they find out later that he isn't like they imagined him. But if the father shows that he cares, sends money, spends time with them and shows a sincere interest, he becomes part of their lives. They can see the real problems he faces, and that way they get a real taste of life through him. I think this can help them mature better as individuals.*

EARL, JR.—You're talking about boys and their fathers?

EARL, SR.—*I'm talking about boys and girls. They both need their fathers. Certainly a boy needs to have a man around to guide him, be a little tough with him, but a girl needs that same guidance. They are forming their opinions, too. If they grow up and think that all men are no good because those are the only kind of men they see, then that's the attitude that they're going to pass on to their children.*

*If they see their father as somebody who's a warm and caring person—I don't mean weak. I think you can be warm, caring and gentle and still be strong. I think that's what's going to come through and that's what girls will pass on.*

EARL, JR.—One last question. Was it tough making it through life with your family?

EARL, SR.—*Oh, your mother and I had our share of problems. Sometimes there wasn't enough money. Sometimes there might be bills that we couldn't pay. There were a few times when we couldn't get enough coal to heat the house properly. And, like I said before, we had plenty of disputes about everything.*

*But I might work a little longer to earn a few more dollars. Your mother was a talented seamstress, so she would make clothes for friends and neighbors, and they would pay her a little something. She would also make clothes for you and your sister. We had friends whom we always tried to do right by, so when we needed a helping hand, they were there.*

*We took you to church, to the doctor and to school. When you were really young, you even slept in our bed with us. We always told you that our house was your house. Whatever we had, you had. We made it clear that whenever you had a problem you could come to us. It didn't make any difference what it was.*

*But the main thing is that your mother and I were a team. We always figured that as long as we worked together the Good Lord would show us a way. And he did.*

---

## GUIDE 18

I challenge my kids. I want them to think for themselves and to accept responsibility for their actions.

# 7

# SURVIVING AMERICA

When I was eight, my father decided that we would drive to California. It was the first trip I had ever made and I was excited. I dreamed of the adventure of seeing strange and fascinating new places. Each evening, as dusk began to settle, my father pulled into a filling station. He took a small blue-covered book from the glove compartment and carefully circled an address in it.

A short time later, we drove to the address he had circled. It might be a small motel at the edge of town, or even a private home. We spent the night there. I later found out that blacks owned these motels or homes. In those days, they were the only places that a black traveller crossing the country could stay.

I did not realize it at the time, but my father was giving me a lesson in the art of black survival. A lesson that life has forced many black fathers to learn.

LAWRENCE—*My family has been my strength. I have always maintained close contact with everyone in my immediate family. It has paid off. There have been times when I have needed help and they have been there. They know that if they need help, I will be there for them.*

African-Americans have always known how to survive. During slavery, blacks took the leftovers from the slave master and made gourmet meals out of them. They took his tattered hand-me-down clothes and made warm garments for their children. The first chance they got, many fled to the swamps and forests or headed North to freedom.

HOWARD—*I knew back then that there was no way that my kids could get the kind of education I wanted for them in the South. The question for me and my wife was not whether we should move, but when and where.*

Men like Absalom Jones and Richard Allen, founders of the African Methodist Episcopal Church, believed that black progress came through mutual aid and support. They made that clear in the preamble of the Free African Society they founded in 1787: "to support one another in sickness, and for the benefit of their widows and fatherless children."

ROBERT—*If anything happens to me, I want my children to be financially secure. I have a trust account that I set up in the names of my sons for college. I have a separate savings account that I try to put a few extra dollars into each month. My plan is to eventually use that money to invest in real estate or a business. Hopefully, the income from that will grow over the years. By the time they are old enough, I will be in an even better position to help them with their education or business training.*

*When I make my deposits, I try to take one of my sons with me so he can see how the savings process works. I want my sons to understand how money is invested and how wealth is accumulated. This way they can manage their own financial future.*

Despite the pain and suffering, African-Americans have been blessed. Their music and humor sustained them. Their extended families protected them. Their colleges educated them. Their churches gave them comfort and guidance. For many, their fathers gave them love.

PERRY—*I want my children to be independent. I want them to be able to stand on their own two feet and face the world. I want them to be able to make it on their own talents and abilities. I don't want them to be obligated to anyone. I want them to be able to provide for their own needs and fulfill their desires. If I can give them that, I will be satisfied that I have done my job as a father who cared and loved them.*

There is an African proverb that says to stumble is not to fall but to go forward faster. Black fathers may not be all that we want, nor all that we hope. They are heroes and villains. They are saints and sinners. They are protectors and abusers. They are pain and joy.

They are men with with all the strengths and weaknesses of other men. They have stumbled, but they have not fallen. "Ain't I a father too?" Certainly. Without our fathers many African-Americans would not have survived America.

---

## GUIDE 19

I want my children to be independent. I want them to be able to stand on their own two feet and face the world. If I can give them that, I will be satisfied that I have done my job as a father who cared and loved them.

# APPENDIX

## Interview Questions

SOME QUESTIONS MAY NOT APPLY. PLEASE TRY TO BE BRIEF AND SPECIFIC WITH THOSE THAT YOU ANSWER. ALSO TRY TO THINK OF A SPECIFIC SITUATION OR CONVERSATION WITH YOUR WIFE OR SIGNIFICANT OTHER TO GO WITH YOUR ANSWER.

### INTRODUCTION: HOW THEY ARE SEEN

1. What are the barriers to black fatherhood?

### CHAPTER 1 — THE CHALLENGE OF BLACK LIFESTYLES

2. What do you do to overcome problems in your relationship with your wife and/or other?

3. How do you provide for your children—the necessities (clothes, food, shelter, etc.) and their development/growth?

4. In what ways do you rely on others (friends, relatives) to help with your children, finances, household affairs, etc.?

5. In what ways do you work with your wife or

significant other in the daily running of the house-hold?

6. What do you do to help your children avoid gangs/violence?

7. What do you do to help your children avoid drugs/alcohol?

### CHAPTER 2 — DON'T LEAVE EDUCATION TO THE SCHOOLS!

8. In what ways do you get involved in your children's education?

9. What do you do to motivate your children to stay in school? Excell in school?

10. How do you make your children (boys especially) understand that studying is more important than sports?

11. How do you help your children select their careers?

### CHAPTER 3 — SEX , HEALTH AND OURSELVES

12. When and how do you educate your children about sex?

13. What do you do to teach your children about safe (or no) sex?

14. What do you do to keep your child healthy?

15. What do you do to instill respect for the opposite sex (boys for girls, girls for boys)?

16. Do you have a responsibility to maintain a relationship only with a black woman?

## CHAPTER 4 — I DIDN'T MAKE THE BABY BY MYSELF

17. What can bring black men that have deserted their homes back?

18. What do you think can prevent separation/divorce?

19. What can a father not in the home do to take care of his children?

20. If you are (or were) a single father what do (did) you do to raise your children alone? And to prepare them to accept a new female in the home?

## CHAPTER 5 — AN AFROCENTRIC PASSAGE TO ADULTHOOD

21. What values of life do you try to instill in your children?

22. In what ways do you instill religious values and belief in God in your children?

23. When and how do you discipline?

24. What is the ideal role model for your children?

## CHAPTER 7 — SURVIVING AMERICA

25. What is your survival strategy for yourself and your family?

# REFERENCES

## INTRODUCTION

P. 1

Harriet Tubman, *The Narrative of Sojourner Truth (1878)* (New York: Arno Press, 1968) 120-121.

P. 1

Ralph Ellison, *Invisible Man* (New York: Vintage Books, 1972) 3.

P. 2

Herbert G. Guttman, *The Black Family in Slavery and Freedom, 1750-1925* (New York: Random House, 1976) 144, 415.

P. 4

The Negro Family: The Case for National Action (Washington: U.S. Government Printing Office, 1965).

P. 5

Dr. Martin Luther King, Jr., *Where Do We Go From Here: Chaos or Community?* (Boston: Beacon Press, 1968) 108.

## Chapter 1

P. 16

Dr. Martin Luther King, Jr., *Where Do We Go From Here: Chaos or Community?* (Boston: Beacon Press, 1968) 197.

P. 20

Joanne Martin & Elmer Martin, *The Helping Tradition in the Black Family* (Silver Springs, Md., 1985) 17.

P. 20

Andrew Billingsley, *Black Families in White America* (Englewood Cliffs, NJ: Prentice Hall, 1968) 39-40.

P. 31

Claude Brown, *Manchild in the Promised Land* (New York: New American Library, 1965) 263.

P. 32

Alex Haley with Malcolm X, *The Autobiography of Malcolm X* (New York: Grove Press, 1964) 263.

## Chapter 3

P. 62

See *The Complete Poems of Paul Laurence Dunbar* (New York: Dodd, Mead, 1975).

P. 63

For the full quote from Fannie Lou Hamer, see *Black Women in White America*, Gerda Lerner, ed. (New York: Pantheon, 1972) 611-612.

## CHAPTER 4

P. 78

Quoted in Joseph W. Scott, "From Teenage Parenthood to Polygamy" in Robert Staples, *The Black Family* (Belmont, Ca.: Wadsworth Publishing Co., 1991) 284.

## CHAPTER 5

P. 86

Alex Haley, *Roots*, (New York: Doubleday, 1976) 80.

P. 97

W.E.B. DuBois, *The Souls of Black Folk* (New York: Fawcett Publications, 1961) 151.

P. 98

Hart M. Nelson, Raytha L. Yokley and Anne K. Nelson, eds., *The Black Church in America*, (New York: Basic Books, 1971) 19.

P. 107

James Baldwin, *Notes of a Native Son* (Boston: Beacon Press, 1955) 105.

## SELECTED BIBLIOGRAPHY

### Books

Clarke, John Henrik, ed., *Harlem: A Community in Transition* (New York: Citadel Press, 1969).

Chu, Daniel, and Skinner, Elliot, *A Glorious Age In Africa* (New York: Doubleday, 1965).

Comer, James P. and Alvin F. Poussaint, *Black Child Care: How to Bring Up a Healthy Black Child in America* (New York: Simon and Shuster, 1975).

Eimers, Robert and Aitchison, Robert, *Effective Parents/Responsible Children* (New York: McGraw-Hill, 1977).

Franklin, John Hope, *From Slavery to Freedom* (New York: Vintage Books, 1969).

Frazier, E. Franklin, *The Negro Family in the United States* (Chicago: The University of Chicago Press, 1966).

Glassgow, Douglas G., *The Black Underclass* (New York: Vintage Books, 1981).

Grant, Joanne, *Black Protest* (New York: Fawcett, 1969).

Greif, Geoffrey L., *The Daddy Track and the Single Father* (Lexington, Mass.: Lexington Books, 1990).

Marone, Nicky, *How to Father a Successful Daughter* (New York: McGraw-Hill, 1988).

National Urban League, *The State of Black America, 1989* (New York: National Urban League, Inc., 1989)

—*The State of Black America, 1990* (New York: National Urban League, Inc., 1990).

Pinkney, Alphonso, *The Myth of Black Progress* (New York: University of Cambridge Press, 1989).

Pruett, Kyle D., *The Nurturing Father* (New York: Warner Books, 1987).

Samalin, Nancy, *Loving Your Child Is Not Enough: Positive Discipline That Works* (New York: Viking, 1987).

Sullivan, S. Adams, *The Father's Almanac* (Garden City, N.Y.: Dolphin, 1980).

Weiss, Joan Solomon, *Raising A Son* (New York: Simon and Schuster, 1985).

## Magazines

Harris, Peter J., "Heroic Fathers," *Essence,* 19 (October, 1988) 162.

Haskins, William J. "What about Teenage Fathers?" *Essence,* 15 (November, 1984) 160.

Leavy, Walter, "Fathers Who Walk Away," *Ebony,* 41 (August, 1986) 61.

Marriott, Michael, "Father Hunger," *Essence,* 21 (November, 1990) 73.

News Column, "Black Men with Educated Fathers Likely to Divorce," *Jet,* 76 (September 18, 1989) 31.

Powell, Gregory, "I'm a Witness to the fact that Good Black Fathers are not Extinct," *Essence,* 17 (March, 1987) 10.

# INDEX

**A**
Abolitionist, 1
Afrocentric passage, 85-87
AIDS, 14, 60-61
African contributions, 20
African spiritualism, 96-97
Alcoholism, 14, 34-35

**B**
Baldwin, James, 108-109
Billingsley, Andrew, 20,
Black colleges, 45
Black educators, 45
Black families, 3
Black pride, 93-94
Black values, 88-89, 91-92
Black survival, 134
Brown, Claude, 31

**C**
Child support, 76

**D**
Discipline, 101-105
Dred Scott decision, 111
Drugs, 14, 30-34
DuBois, W.E.B., 97
Dunbar, Paul Laurence, 62

**E**
Education, 37-41
Edwards, Harry, 45-47
Ellison, Ralph, 1
Extended black family, 20-22

**F**
Fatherhood, 2

**G**
Gangs, 14, 30
Garvey, Marcus, 95

**H**
Haley, Alex, 86
Hamer, Fannie Lou, 63
Health, 58-69
HIV, 60-61

**I**
Interracial marriage, 67-70

**J**
Job Discrimination, 52

**K**
King, Martin Luther, Jr., 5, 16, 26

**M**
Malcolm X, 32-33, 84
Marriage, 3-4, 14
Moynihan, Daniel Patrick, 4-5

**P**
Poverty, 17, 56

**R**
Randolph, A. Phillip, 26
Relationships, 15-16, 36, 66-68
Religion, 97-99
Respect, 62-65, 104
Rite of Passage, 85-87
Role models, 105-107

**S**
Sex education, 54-58
Segregation, 52
Single fathers, 80-81
Single mother, 72-74, 78
Slavery, 52-53, 134
Sports, 45-50

**T**
Truth, Sojourner, 1

**V**
Violence, 14
Values, 88-89, 91-92

**W**
Wilde, Oscar, 110
Work, women, 22-25